ARCHITECTURAL ELEMENTS

Architectural Elements
The Technological Revolution

Galvanized iron roof plates and corrugated sheets; cast iron facades, columns, door and window caps, sills and lintels; galvanized cornices; marbleized slate mantels; plumbing and heating supplies and fixtures; staircases, balconies, newels and balusters in wood and iron; cut and etched glass transoms and sidelights

Edited, and with an Introduction by Diana S. Waite

AMERICAN HISTORICAL CATALOG COLLECTION

THE PYNE PRESS
Princeton

First edition
Library of Congress Catalog Card Number 72-95727

SBN 87861-043-X, paperbound edition
SBN 87861-042-1, hardcover edition

Catalog material used in assembling *Architectural Elements*, Marshall Lefferts & Brother and Morris, Tasker & Co., courtesy of Baker Library, Harvard University; Buffalo Eagle Iron Works, Keystone Mantel & Slate Works, and Philadelphia Architectural Iron Co., courtesy of Smithsonian Institution Libraries; George O. Stevens, courtesy of Virginia Historical Landmarks Commission

Manufactured in the United States of America

Distributed by Charles Scribner's Sons

Architectural Elements
an historical introduction

*The low price of manufactured work has induced
a great many farmers and other persons, who
formerly lived in log cabins, to build good,
comfortable houses; and capitalists in our cities
have found out that buildings made in this
way can be erected and rented so as to pay
from ten to twenty per cent on the cost.*

Thus in their 1862 catalog, Hinkle, Guild & Co. of Cincinnati, who had been fabricating building materials since 1845, described their contribution to the growth of America. What they were describing was, in effect, a revolution in building techniques, for until the nineteenth century building materials had been consistently worked in the same manner, by hand. The six catalogs reproduced here document that revolution and the extent to which standardized building components had become generally available by mid-century. The range included some of the smallest and simplest elements, like roofing plates, and others much larger and more complex, such as the entire fronts of buildings, encompassing materials that were used in a building's structural and mechanical systems as well as in its decorative finish. There is nothing very revolutionary about the *actual* products described. By the time such catalogs were distributed, the products they offered—in iron, sheet metal, glass, wood and slate—had been well tested through long and extensive use. Indeed, the manufacturers devoted considerable space to testimonials and lists of awards and of structures in which their products had been used to convey just that impression. Thus the catalogs illustrate in very concrete terms how comprehensive the mass production of building components had become. If they appear startling and remarkable to us, it is because of our ignorance of the history of both the trade catalog and the manufacture of building materials, not because the catalogs or the materials were uncommon in their day.

The catalogs both reflect and helped form the American culture of the mid-nineteenth century. They were a product of new systems of transportation and industrialization and of population growth. Without these conditions there would have been no mass-produced products to offer nor, on the other hand, great demand for them. At the same time the products advertised in these pages had an important effect on vernacular building methods and styles.

Central to America's material growth during the nineteenth century was the expansion of networks of rail and waterways, which provided speedy and efficient means of moving raw materials and finished products to and from the sources of supply and demand. Simultaneously, the growing population (which had more than tripled between 1830 and 1860) was enlarging older urban areas and spreading to the western territories. The need for housing and for new buildings in which to manufacture and distribute the goods required by this population was tremendous. The answer lay not with traditional craftsmanship but in the industrialization of the building process.

This transformation occurred largely in the cities, and it is surely not a coincidence that the trade catalogs reproduced here emanated from such great metropolitan centers as New York, Philadelphia and Baltimore. The greatest demand for building materials was urban, for between 1820 and 1860 the growth of the cities was greater than the force of western migration, but the railroads and waterways also delivered the finished products to this second market. The building materials catalog was a critical link in this new production and distribution system, essential to informing builders, engineers, and architects of the nature and reputation of not just the materials

5

but the firm itself. The catalog was intended for distant buyers ("it greets you as our traveling man and solicitor—the only one we employ," stated one) as well as for customers in the same area, since rapid growth had made dependence upon word-of-mouth recommendations difficult. Like the products, the ordering procedure was highly standardized through a numbering system for identifying particular items and by estimators at the home office who calculated costs. A few firms employed intermediary agents or maintained branch offices in major cities, but most depended upon orders received directly from the buyer.

Yet even given vast quantities of raw materials and centralized labor pools, the demands of the market could not have been met without new manufacturing methods, to produce quality materials not only cheaply but also quickly and in quantity. And it was only when those conditions were met that the products of the centralized factory could compete with those of the craftsman and the smaller local firm. The key was the development of a new manufacturing technology based on power machinery, run usually by steam, sometimes by water, that operated within the factory system. This was an era noted for translating scientific knowledge into concrete procedures, and America with her seemingly inexhaustible stock of raw materials, hampered from exploitation only by chronically inadequate sources of labor, was the natural site for this development. To take one example related to these catalogs, the patents for power woodworking machinery inventions were claimed first in England, but it was in America that the machinery was produced and perfected to withstand factory usage.

Mechanization profoundly changed the role of the craftsman engaged in the building trades. Much as the invention of the balloon frame had enabled less-skilled workmen to erect substantial buildings in record time, as compared with the earlier mortise-and-tenon system that could be built only by expert carpenters, the availability of other standardized building components was responsible for transforming the complicated art of building into a trade. The housewright, who had the skills to construct a building from start to finish, was replaced by workmen who were proficient in only one trade. Building became a matter of assembly, and the trade catalogs often included large-scale illustrations or written directions for putting the parts together.

Manufactured components also had a great visual effect upon the buildings and the cities in which they were used, for hand-in-hand with the industrialized manufacture of parts came the standardization of designs. While iron could be cast in a countless number of forms, for window caps, for example, there was a limit to the number of styles and sizes that the iron founder could afford to keep on hand. One result was, of course, a harmony of materials, but there was also a resultant unity of size and scale of architectural elements.

Furthermore, industry responded to changing nineteenth-century tastes by producing the more intricate designs that were desired. This meant that similar designs could be made available simultaneously across the country at reasonable cost. Manufactured components thus were capable of providing a basic level of design sophistication even in frontier areas.

Theoretically, at least, this also meant that the latest styles would also become available simultaneously, with trade catalogs being the means of rapid communication, and in fact most catalogs did prominently point out their new designs. But, significantly, these patterns could hardly be called high style; one suspects from their comparatively conservative nature that they had already proved somewhat popular. Nearly all catalogs presented their newer offerings side-by-side, often literally, with others that had come into vogue a decade, or sometimes two or three, earlier. This very common characteristic dramatically points out the problems and dangers of dating buildings primarily on stylistic evidence.

Along with the builder and engineer, catalog copy indicates the architect was considered a prime market for manufactured building components. But preliminary research suggests that architects played a small role in supplying the designs for mass production at this time (nearly all firms advertised that they would do custom work, but that is a different matter). Most designs, therefore, probably originated with the maker of the patterns for iron castings and sheet metal dies or with the maker of woodworking machinery. This theory is supported by the fact that one can find different companies widely separated in time and location producing identical items.

The trade catalog provides fresh insights into vernacular materials and construction techniques that made established building types accessible to the general population and thus contributed to the rapid urbanization of America. Unlike those of preceding decades, building designs of the mid-nineteenth century were no longer limited mainly to the knowledge and ability of the local housewright. The industrialization of the building process enabled the growing middle class to erect structures in almost any style and variety of forms. By mid-century builders' guides and pattern books were being challenged as the only vocabularies of design by the building materials catalog, which for much of the country was to become the most accessible architectural source. Industrialization thus made possible the realization of many ideals of American democracy by allowing the growing middle class to enjoy the profusion of embellishment and generosity of scale that characterized the architectural taste of the times. Industrialization also contributed to real improvements in the quality of life brought about through the adoption of mechanical systems—heating, lighting, plumbing and ventilation. Since their pages provide irreplaceable evidence of how the Industrial Revolution touched the lives of the masses, the conservation of catalogs such as these and—more important—the preservation of buildings in which use was made of these products are essential to an understanding of nineteenth-century American history and architecture.

The firm of Marshall Lefferts & Brother, importers and manufacturers of patent galvanized iron, had its beginnings in 1852, when their product had become quite widely known and was gaining public acceptance in America. Even so, the Lefferts firm in their first catalog, published in 1852, explained prominently that galvanized iron was the "cheapest and most durable material" for all "purposes where iron is exposed to oxidation and rust, also for all purposes where lead, tin, or zinc has heretofore been used." Furthermore, several pages of testimonial letters were included in both the 1852 and 1854 catalogs, not to commend the firm, but to establish the credibility of the material. Coating iron with zinc was first suggested during the mid-eighteenth century, but galvanizing was not developed into an industrial process until 1836, by the French chemist I. M. Sorel, who obtained a French patent in 1837. Sorel's patent claimed five different methods of coating, but only one was used for building materials, that called "hot-dip" galvanizing. In this process, an alloy of zinc and iron is formed at the surface of the iron, and it is this oxide that gives the galvanized iron the property of resisting oxidation, not simply the zinc coating, as is the case with the tin coating of tinplate. Even today, most galvanizing is done by the basic "hot-dip" method developed by Sorel. Meanwhile, in 1838 it had been discovered that certain metals could be deposited upon others by the use of electric current. When, about 1844, such an application was made in depositing zinc on iron, called electro-galvanizing, it was hailed for "its simplicity, the absence of all injurious effect upon the iron, and the securing a coating of *pure* zinc." While providing for uniform thin coatings of zinc, this technique did not permit the deposit of thick coats, and in 1861 an American writer remarked that the use of galvanic current had been dispensed with in the preparation of galvanized iron.

Various nineteenth-century sources refer to galvanized *tinned* iron as well as to galvanized iron, and the 1852 Lefferts catalog clearly specifies the tinned product, mentioning "tin and zinc, as separate and distinct coatings." Sorel had suggested in 1837 that a coating of tin be applied after galvanizing "to give a brighter and more handsome surface than zinc affords," but Lefferts mentions only the utilitarian advantage of increased durability. However, in the 1854 catalog he refers simply to galvanized iron, and one wonders whether the tinning step had been eliminated in the interval, and if so, why.

In both 1852 and 1854 Lefferts offered flat as well as corrugated galvanized roofing sheets. Flat iron sheets (not galvanized) had been rolled at the end of the eighteenth century and used in America by the opening of the nineteenth century. Corrugating had been invented in England about 1828, and within the next five years corrugated sheets had been used for the roofing of London docks. J. C. Loudon's *Encyclopedia of Cottage, Farm and Villa Architecture*, 1833, considered corrugated iron particularly appropriate for larger cottages, "smithies, carpenters' shops, and all manner of sheds," as well as for portable houses, but warned that "wherever such houses may be erected, they must be covered with ivy, or some other evergreen creeper, to moderate the effect of changes in the exterior temperature."

In 1852 Lefferts outlined the extent to which galvanized plates were then being used and commented upon their advantages over other common roofing materials:

> In this country attention has been chiefly directed to the galvanized tinned iron for roofing, guttering and spouting, and for these purposes the sales are now very large. In our own and neighboring cities, most of the finest buildings are covered with this material; and for reference we would mention the Merchants' Exchange, New York Post Office, Brooklyn City Hall, Grace Church, the magnificent store of A. T. Stewart & Co., Broadway — all the stores of the Atlantic Dock Co., besides a great number of splendid private residences . . . roofs and other works so protected will be found in nearly every principal city in the Union.
>
> The peculiar properties and advantages of the patent galvanized tinned plates consist in their great strength and durability — in their malleability, and especially in the fact that they are PROOF AGAINST RUST — costing less than half as much as copper, and possessing all the good qualities of that expensive metal. They will remain an indefinite length of time unimpaired by the weather, as well upon the seaboard as in the interior; contracting and expanding very slightly from changes of temperature, they will not crack or leak like zinc or tin. They never require paint, like the ordinary tinned plate, and consequently are cooler in summer.

Testimonial letters appearing in the catalogs provide information on some of the earliest uses of galvanized iron. One of the first was in the roof and leaders of the Merchants' Exchange in New York, whose architect, Owen G. Warren, remarked in 1847 that he had been "in the habit of noticing them" since about 1839. The chairman of the Building Committee for the Merchant's Exchange reported in 1842 that he was acquainted with galvanized iron which had been installed in other buildings for three years. Peter Naylor, a leading New York City metal roofer, wrote to Lefferts in April, 1852, regarding galvanized iron that "I have now been in the habit of using it constantly for the last twelve years, and for seven years have employed it almost exclusively in all my work." And it was apparently sufficiently well known and widely distributed for Edward Shaw to recommend in 1843 in the pattern book *Rural Architecture* that roofs "be covered with galvanized iron or tin." These examples all evidently refer to the use of flat plates.

Since corrugating iron plates made them much stiffer and stronger, roof framing could be lightened when a lighter gauge sheet was employed or eliminated when the sheet was curved. In 1852 Lefferts wrote that "Corrugated Galvanized Iron is now being largely used, and possesses advantages which we have not heretofore enjoyed in roofing. — The form of corrugating gives so much strength to the sheet, that the roof requires no boarding — the ends of the sheets resting simply upon rafters" and illustrated this procedure in the 1854 catalog. Corrugated sheets were widely used by both British and American manufacturers (including Peter Naylor) in making prefabricated portable houses that were shipped to California during the Gold Rush. Lefferts pointed out another application to prospective customers in 1852:

> There is now being constructed under orders of the United States Government, CORRUGATED GALVANIZED IRON HOUSES, to be stationed on our Atlantic coast, in which is kept the lifeboat, and all life-saving apparatus, and which in case of shipwreck affords immediate and com-

fortable shelter for the unfortunate people. There can be no better evidence given of the high esteem in which the Galvanized Iron is held by government than their adopting it for such an exposed situation, where common iron would last but a very few months.

As a leading historian, Charles E. Peterson, has commented, galvanized iron has since become one of the classic roofs in this country and "still persists as one of the most practical—if not the most beautiful—American roofs."

When the Buffalo Eagle Iron Works Company entered into the manufacture of architectural cast iron in 1854, the material was in its heyday in America. Cast iron columns combined with timber beams had already been widely utilized in industrial and commercial construction, and first-story iron fronts had been used in New York as early as 1835. In 1849 James Bogardus had patented his system of "Construction of the Frame, Roof, and Floor of Iron Buildings," and the next year completed the first building constructed entirely of cast iron. At about the same time Daniel Badger began casting iron fronts at the Architectural Iron Works of the City of New York.

These structures, along with the others that soon followed, served to dispel many of the fears and prejudices regarding the use of cast iron in construction, but in the literature of the day, even up through the 1870's, proponents of cast iron still seemed to feel the need to refute critics, although their arguments were usually presented as a list of advantages of the material, as evidenced by this writer in 1876:

> For building purposes, cast iron possesses unequalled advantages of strength, durability, economy, and adaptibility to ornament and decoration. In resisting any kind of strain, it is vastly superior to granite, marble, sandstone, or brick. Practically, cast iron is crushing proof, for a column must be ten miles in height before it will crush itself with its own weight. Unlike wrought iron and steel, it is not subject to rapid oxidation and decay by exposure to the atmosphere, and whatever tendency it may have in that direction can easily be prevented by a proper coating of paint.

Furthermore, the intrinsic repetitive nature and relative speed of the casting process made iron components not only comparatively inexpensive but also especially suitable to the buildings of a rapidly growing country. The supposed incombustible nature of cast iron also recommended its use in dense urban commercial areas.

In this context, it is especially interesting to note that the proprietors of the Buffalo Eagle Iron Works, even in their first catalog, published in 1854, made no attempt to convince the skeptic of the material's advantages, except to predict that "the improved appearance of Iron over Stone must secure the general adoption of Iron for Dwelling-houses as well as for Stores and Public Buildings." It seemed rather to be their desire to convince prospective buyers that their selection formed "the most extensive and varied assortment of patterns for Building Castings in the western country," and that they were "continually making new ones."

While each type of architectural component cast by the Eagle Iron Works was also manufactured by Daniel Badger's Architectural Iron Works, the latter offered in addition many other items, such as cornices, railings, and stair risers and treads, as might be expected from such a large, metropolitan firm, One of the greatest differences was that the Buffalo foundry did not advertise what is today commonly termed an iron front, an entire multi-story facade constructed exclusively of iron and glass. Instead, the Buffalo firm's iron fronts were restricted to first-story use, with upper stories having masonry walls trimmed with cast iron sills and caps, as illustrated on page 6 of their catalog. This building type proved very adaptable to mercantile and industrial purposes, for it had many advantages. The strength of cast iron allowed large first-story windows. The ornamental detail of the fronts could be reproduced inexpensively and with remarkable resemblance to stone. And unlike porous stone, iron fronts needed only a fresh coat of paint to look new. Builders of brick front rowhouses also often used cast iron door and window sills and lintels.

By 1859 the Eagle Iron Works had also introduced two designs for "grating to go under window," used as spandrels beneath the first story sills of iron facades (page 32). Curiously, these designs are identical with two "Lattice Pannels" of the same function in plate 57 of Daniel Badger's catalog of 1865, which encourages speculation about interconnections between these and other firms and about the source of the wooden patterns used in casting. Since its founding the Eagle Iron Works had also offered iron fronts with the "Patent Fire Proof Rolling Shutters . . . now so generally used in New York" that were so prominently illustrated by Badger. Furthermore, by 1865 Badger had erected four iron store fronts in Buffalo, so the proprietors of Buffalo Eagle Iron must have been acquainted with Badger's work.

Various nineteenth-century commentators praised this use of cast iron, like Benson J. Lossing, who wrote: "By the use of this cheap material in skilled hands, forms of beauty have multiplied, and made familiar to the common eye, and a wide-spread cultivation of artistic taste has been the consequence." There was, however, a rising tide of criticism about the way cast iron was utilized to imitate forms that were appropriate to stone and of the lack of taste evidenced by some designers, in "overloading the surface with poorly executed ornament [that] gave their structures a flashy and vulgar appearance." But William J. Fryer, commenting in 1876, noted further that "these early stages have been passed, and taste and utility now go hand in hand."

The Morris, Tasker & Co. catalog of 1860 is especially interesting in comparison with the others in this collection, for the firm manufactured not only structural and ornamental iron building parts but also many components of the mechanical systems of buildings that became essential to urban expansion. Within fifty years the firm grew from a stove foundry to America's most extensive and complete manufactory of wrought-iron pipes. By 1878, the company reportedly made "every variety of apparatus required to light, heat, ventilate, or supply with gas or water buildings of every description," many of which are shown on their catalog cover.

Morris, Tasker & Co. first began manufacturing pipe about 1836, when the Philadelphia Gas Works, the first American municipal gas system, commenced operations. During that year the firm made 60,000 feet of gas tubing. The impetus for engaging in this business had been provided by a pipe maker who had recently arrived in Philadelphia from England, where wrought iron pipes had been introduced in 1825 to supply London gas customers. During the 1840's and 1850's gas companies were formed throughout the United States, and by 1860 gas had become the principal means of artificial lighting in every large American city.

Concurrently, Morris, Tasker & Co. expanded their line of manufacture to meet other needs of this new business. By 1872 it was reported that "the establishment possesses the most ample facilities for erecting gas-works complete from the very beginning, the retorts and buildings involved, to the gas-holders for storing the gas; for the pipes for supplying and distributing it from the works to the house of the consumer, with all the variety of fittings of cast or wrought-iron which can be imagined, with the tools for the gas-fitter's trade." The cover of their 1860 catalog includes an illustration of an iron gasholder which rose and fell according to the amount of gas being stored in it by means of a system of pulleys and rails. Also shown are gas lights for street use. While the firm made cast iron pipe as well, their speciality was welded wrought iron pipe.

Meanwhile, municipal water systems were being introduced in American cities and towns. By 1860, the year of this catalog, 136 water works companies had been established. Cast iron water mains and smaller pipes such as those made by Morris, Tasker & Co. gradually replaced the early mains of wooden logs and lead interior plumbing.

Closely related to this production was the firm's manufacture of fire hydrants, sewer inlets, vault covers, and plumbing fixtures. The illustration showing full bathrooms on each floor of a multi-story urban building is particularly noteworthy, for it dates from just before the "French flats" controversy concerning the propriety of housing more than one family under one roof and because this type of layout was not then common. In the more elegant hotels and well-to-do town-houses, complete bathrooms were becoming standard features, but it was not until the 1880's that full bathrooms began to appear regularly in more modest homes. The Morris, Tasker & Co. fixtures are particularly interesting because they clearly show spigots for not just cold but hot water. The general adoption of plumbing was closely tied to the standardization of fittings between pipes and outlets to replace those hand-crafted of lead by plumbers, and Morris, Tasker & Co. was apparently also a leader in this field. They also made slop hoppers, soil pans, various traps and valves, and hot water heating coils.

The firm was evidently quite progressive in the heating business as well. One of the founders, Thomas T. Tasker, was the inventor of a self-regulating hot water furnace and also a gravity steam system of heating.

They also put out several patterns of steam radiators ranging from simple styles suitable for industrial buildings and for drying closets to boldly ornamental styles for both manifold and pedestal types. Somewhat less pretentious were the "ornamental cases" for radiators, while the designs of the screens and ventilator fronts were relatively subdued. Like indoor plumbing, the common adoption of steam heating was a later nineteenth-century phenomenon: in 1840 the business amounted to only $200,000 per year; by 1860 it had increased tenfold, and by 1880 it had grown to $15,000,000 annually. Morris, Tasker & Co. also made a line of dampers, flues, doors, and oven dampers.

The firm also handled a line of cast iron architectural elements of varying functions, including circular stairs, foot scrapers, and richly ornamented mantel and balcony brackets. Also shown are cast iron columns ranging from very simple ones with round shafts and simply moulded capitals to fluted examples with capitals inspired by Corinthian and Egyptian motifs.

The changes that occurred in the galvanized sheet iron business in the years following Marshall Lefferts and Brother's catalog are well illustrated by the catalog issued by the *Philadelphia Architectural Iron Works* in 1872. There are some striking similarities between the two publications, especially in the roof framing systems and the suggested covering of corrugated sheet iron. A roof of curved corrugated iron is shown by the Philadelphia firm, strengthened only by tie rods and braces, not a very different system from the tie rods suggested by Lefferts in 1854. Both firms also made galvanized gutters.

By the 1870's galvanized sheet metal, as it was then called, was being used in imitation of wood and stone architectural elements, chiefly for cornices and other trim. Initially cornices were turned out in six foot lengths, but later machinery for making eight and ten foot lengths was introduced. Sheet metal was more resistant to rot than wood and was also fireproof, a factor that contributed greatly to its popularity after new building codes, adopted in the 1860's and later, prohibited the use of wooden cornices and Mansard roofs. Compared with stone, sheet metal was also relatively lightweight, which made it particularly suitable, as one manufacturer explained, "in our large cities where there is so much made land, the foundation not being solid enough to support the immense weight put upon it, and causing the walls to settle," a claim that also seems to suggest a somewhat questionable future for the whole building. The Architectural Iron Works had manufactured galvanized cornices for twenty years and mentioned in the catalog how during this interval they had "gradually but surely" gained public favor. The company listed the "primary merit" of galvanized cornices as cheapness not only in initial installation (about one-third the cost of stone) but also in replacement if damaged. It was, furthermore, durable and strong, but could be manipulated easily. Its intrinsic quality of readily taking the impression of dies made it adaptable to any number of designs, a small variety of which are illustrated in the cornices and smaller stamped ornaments of this catalog.

11

At the Centennial Exposition of 1876 Kittredge & Co., an Ohio firm, erected a small sheet metal pavilion to display cornices and other stamped sheet metal work. The *American Architect and Building News* promptly denounced the structure as "perhaps the most offensive building in the grounds," which was "loaded with coarse ornament of the most pretentious kind." These statements touched off a debate between a Philadelphia sheet metal manufacturer, who signed himself "Quaker," and the magazine's editors serving to illuminate many of the objections architects and others had to the material.

The editors agreed with "Quaker" that galvanized sheet metal was a useful and valuable building material that could satisfactorily be used in such components as grilles, gates, railings, roof coverings and ornaments, which could not be made well in stone. Their arguments were couched mainly in aesthetic terms, centering on the position that the use of any building material should reflect, not disguise, its good qualities and that a material should not be used where another was more appropriate in terms of its inherent physical qualities.

"Quaker," on the other hand, argued that it was the outline and the immediate surface qualities that were the important features in architectural ornament and that they could be conveyed as effectively in sheet metal as in stone. He also presented the rather questionable argument that it was a "wanton waste of the people's money to insist that the costlier embellishments must be in stone," when with a few exceptions "even the largest structures are not permitted to stand, at the outside, but fifty to seventy-five years." (This position is quite opposite that presented in the Lefferts catalog where architects were encouraged to use galvanized iron because "it is time for American architects to think of posterity, and to regard perpetuity as an object of consideration.") "Quaker" countered further that those attacking the aesthetic qualities of his products could be of service by putting what they considered appropriate designs to paper, but the editors replied that the sheet metal fabricators would do well to employ well-trained and skillful architects to execute designs for them.

Richard Morris Hunt in reporting on the architectural exhibits of the Centennial was somewhat more gracious when he commented (surely tongue-in-cheek) that "the artisans working these sheet-metals have from the beginning displayed great ingenuity in producing work at small expense and proportionately durable, copying the traditional forms of stonework to perfection. The galvanized-iron pavilion represents very fully the achievements of the trade in the country." He closed by remarking that "the tendency to return to the legitimate use of stone for cornices, limiting the use of sheet-metals to such portions of the roof as cresting, hips, gutter-linings, etc., is to be welcomed with satisfaction."

Galvanized sheet metal, however, did continue to be widely used for cornices, so much so that one writer commented in 1891 that in deciding upon a cornice the question was not "of what material shall the cornice be made . . . but rather how shall the cornice be proportioned, constructed or designed . . . the assumption being that, of course, it will be of sheet metal." By this time, however, the durability of the material was being questioned, and it was recommended that it be painted regularly. But the "infinite suggestion of utilities" predicted in 1843 had been at least partially realized.

The art of coloring surfaces to resemble marble, commonly called marbling or marbleizing, which had been known at least since the time of the Roman Empire, was extensively revived during the nineteenth century for interior decoration, especially for wall coverings and for the decoration of slate, chiefly mantels. Prior to its introduction in America, marbleized slate had been known in Europe for some time. A New York firm advertised in 1859 that "Marbleized Slate-Stone Mantels, have been used in Europe, and highly approved, for the last ninety years," while a Troy company noted in 1867 that they had been "used and highly approved of in Europe for the last twenty years."

The marbleized slate industry in America did not develop until slate quarries had been opened and railroad lines built to transport the material cheaply. Some attempts were made to quarry slate in Pennsylvania as early as the 1760's, but it was not until the mid-1840's that extensive quarrying was undertaken there in York, Lehigh, and Northampton counties. Meanwhile, quarries had been opened in Vermont and Maine in 1839. But the greatest expansion occurred during the 1850's when the number of quarries increased from five to 22. Previously nearly all slate used in America had been imported and limited to use largely in the seaport cities, because of the expense involved in shipping it into the interior. By 1866 the rapidly growing American market for slate was fully supplied by domestic quarries, and before the end of the century slate was being exported.

The great majority of the American quarries had been opened primarily to obtain slate for roofing purposes and, to a lesser extent, for schoolroom blackboards. Slate which did not have the proper physical characteristics for these purposes was used as slabs, but in some instances quarries were worked chiefly for slab slate. One Lehigh County quarry, for example, opened primarily to obtain slate for mantels and blackboards, was, in fact, called the Mantel Quarry.

Wilson & Miller asserted in their Keystone Mantel catalog of 1874 that in 1853 they had been the first to introduce marbleized slate mantels in Pennsylvania. These, however, had been manufactured in New England, where reportedly they were first introduced a year or two earlier; and it was not until after 1856 that the Philadelphia firm began manufacturing mantels.

The marbleizing technique, which was carried out at the quarry or at a city mantel-works, was described thus in *Knight's American Mechanical Dictionary* in 1884 and was the same process that had been used during the preceding decades:

> The slab is rubbed with pumice, and then polished with pulverized pumice and afterward with felt. It is then painted with the groundwork color, and its surface dipped in a vat containing water, on which oil-colors have been sprinkled, manipulated with a brush and subjected to a fanning process, in order to cause a variegated appearance.
>
> Imitations of various kinds of marble are produced by an appropriate application of the different colors. Successive bakings and polishings complete the process.

A coat of varnish was often applied as the last step. Soiled marble could be "remarbled" in this way. Firms boasted that they could reproduce marbles of "every variety now in use," and one company listed 21 as being "a few" of those available. According to Wilson & Miller, the most desired were Spanish, Egyptian, and Verde Antique, whose popularity continued through at least the next decade. The other marbleized slate items that Keystone Mantel offered for sale—fireboards, furniture tops, brackets and bracket shelves, chessboards, register facings, pedestals and columns for statuary, wainscoating, and baseboards—were typical of those offered by other firms during this period. Pulpits and marbleized bases for kerosene lamps were also made. A Buffalo dealer claimed to be "the inventor of the Marbleized Slate Casket, which is elegant in construction and imperishable in its nature," but caskets had been made in Vermont even earlier. Like those of other firms, the Wilson & Miller catalog also included slate sinks, bathtubs, wash tubs, paving, and tiles, but is unclear as to whether all these were also marbleized.

The finished product was heralded by many as being "so closely imitated as to defy detection" and as being unquestionably beautiful:

> The business is one that combines beauty with utility, and the artistic design and finish of the goods manufactured are chaste and beautiful in the highest degree, and when fitted up, impart a palatial appearance of splendour to the apartments, which is truly magnificent. Marbleized Base Boards and Wainscoating in Panel for parlors, dining and drawings-rooms, also for stairways, etc., conveys a degree of elegance to the residence that cannot be approached or imitated by anything else in the way of ornament or decorative art.

A New York firm even claimed that in the marbleizing process the slate was actually converted into marble!

In presenting their revised catalog of 1872 Wilson & Miller declared that they deemed it "unnecessary to go into an elaborate treatise" on the uses and advantages of marbleized slate, but other firms commonly expounded upon its virtues at great lengths, especially its advantages over marble. This description taken from a catalog published about 1876 is not atypical:

> How dingy an old marble mantel looks! The yellow smoky appearance offends the *eye* and takes away *all* the beauty of *design* and *workmanship*, however elaborate. A *Slate Mantel* costs at least 30 *per cent less;* always looks *bright*, being polished to a high degree; the colors are durable, cheerful; *the Mantel lasts a lifetime.*

Manufacturers also claimed that, unlike marble, slate mantels would not be stained by smoke, coal gas, oil or acids, while other makers pointed out that mantels should not be considered luxuries, because they were actually "the most economical article of household furniture ever offered to the public." Another advantage, and one that was especially relevant to the mail-order business, was that slate was several times stronger than marble (a fact that some attributed to heating the slate during marbleizing) and could consequently be shipped with much less chance of breakage.

While marbleized mantels had been manufactured by several firms in the 1850's and were quite widely distributed by that time (they were available as far west as St. Louis by 1859), their period of greatest popularity appears to have been during the late 1860's and 1870's. During the 1870's a rash of advertisements, commonly illustrated with a mantel and accompanied by a listing of the marbles that could be imitated, appeared in numerous city directories and other mercantile publications. It was claimed in 1875 that "comparatively few mantels of the pure marble" were then made, and in the Census of 1880 marbleized mantel firms had attained enough significance to be listed along with the makers of marble ones. The extent of their use was described in glowing terms in this statement made about 1876:

> Slate Mantels can now be found from parlor to attic, not only in the palatial residences of the banker and merchant prince, but also in the less pretentious but equally refined homes of those less favored by fortune. FARMERS throughout the country; *mechanics* or tradesmen, in suburban towns and villages, in building new houses are, in nearly *all* cases, purchasing *Slate* Mantels. In remodelling their dwellings, they remove the *old-fashioned*, ill-shaped, wooden mantels of "ye olden time," replacing them with Slate Mantels, specially designed *to match their own selections* of carpets, trimmings, or decorations....

The ready availability of the raw material does not alone explain why marbleized mantels so quickly gained public favor. Their lower cost and considerably superior physical qualities over marble were contributing factors. But equally important was the steadily increasing demand for a wider variety of colored marbles and inlaid designs which were rapidly becoming essential features of architectural embellishment in the creation of the polychrome interior.

Marbleizing and its counterpart, graining, did not, of course, meet with unqualified support from all. John Ruskin had a great influence upon the practice of falsely representing building materials, and especially condemned "above all, the green and yellow sickness of the false marble." The increasing preference for hardwood mantels also affected the demand for slate. But during the 1920's both graining and marbling underwent what was termed a "deserved revival," and as late as 1933 marbleized mantels were still being produced in Pennsylvania, but by a technique that involved photography.

The materials offered for sale in the 1879 catalog of *George O. Stevens & Co.* of Baltimore were produced by the sophisticated power woodworking machinery that had been invented primarily in England but perfected for factory use in America. The prerequisite to this had been the development of the power sawmill that made possible the transformation of logs into lumber in large quantities. Shortly after American woodworking machinery was exhibited at the Crystal Palace Exhibition held in London in 1851, the United States was acknowledged as "the natural home and native land of this kind of machinery" and retained that position for at least several decades. At the Centennial Exposition of 1876 American woodworking tools were hailed for their "great refinement, accuracy, fitness for their intended purpose, balanced spindles, and minute attention given to truth in the details." But the power woodworking industry was roundly criticized at home and abroad for wasteful use of lumber.

While Stevens advertised as a dealer in building supplies, his factory was derived from a sash and blind factory, an important American industry whose history has not been extensively studied. A very early sash and blind factory was in operation in Camillus, New York, by 1817. Another, located in Troy, reported in 1830 that it had "made last year 28,500 lights of sash, and employed 2 men," figures that indicate that power machinery must have been in use. In 1847 during its first year of operation a Cohoes, New York, establishment employing "from 6 to 8 men" enjoyed "facilities for making sash for 50 windows per day, and a proportionate number of venetian shutter blinds." By 1855 in New York State alone 200 sash and blind factories were in operation.

Sometimes a planing mill also made sash and blinds, but more frequently they were separate factories. Succeeding years saw increased specialization within wood-working establishments. There were also combined planing and moulding mills, as well as turning companies, and turning and scroll sawing establishments — all of which made some of the items shown in the Stevens catalog. In 1850 sash and blind factories first received separate listings in the United States Census. At that time there were 433 factories nationwide, employing 2500 hands. By 1870 there was a total of 1605 factories engaging 20,379 workers. By 1880 the number had been reduced to 1288, but the number of laborers, amount of capital invested, and the value of the finished products were nearly identical.

These firms manufactured finished wood products that were very different from those of ordinary planing mills, which turned out rougher lumber. They used very specialized machinery run chiefly by steam but also by water power (the 1870 Census reported 999 steam engines and 387 water wheels then being used in sash and blind factories). An inventory of a Washington, D.C., factory taken in 1865 indicates that the following machines of varying vintages were then in the factory: two circular saws, two cross-cut saws, one scroll saw, two blind slat machines, one boring machine, four mortising machines, one sash sticker, one tenoning machine, two moulding machines, two planing machines, and one lathe.

Stevens' firm was well located to receive raw materials. When he first went into business in 1855, the center of the lumber industry was shifting from Maine and New York south to central Pennsylvania, whence the white pine and hemlock logs and milled lumber were floated down the Susquehanna River to Baltimore. The Midwest and South supplied large quantities of poplar, ash, white and yellow pine, and walnut. From Baltimore the milled products were transported to the southern states and as far as South America and the West Indies. The Stevens' catalog dates from a very prosperous era in the Baltimore sash and blind business, which reached its apex about 1880 after a period of very rapid expansion in the late 1860's and early 1870's.

With the advent of woodworking machinery capable of producing complex architectural elements, even owners of modest means could have elaborately carved and moulded woodwork both inside and outside their homes and places of work, as was noted in 1873: "so great have been the advances in this department of industry, that the humblest and cheapest dwelling erected in the larger cities at this present writing, will compare favorably in the interior finish with the most gorgeous edifices of former times." Through improved transportation systems and the trade catalog these manufactures were equally available to the country dweller; the particular Stevens catalog reproduced here was once owned by a resident of rural Louisa, Va. While claims were made that machine-made woodwork could surpass hand-made work "as regards accuracy, perfection of finish and durability," it did not meet with unreserved enthusiasm from all sides, as acknowledged by one manufacturer in the 1860's:

> Many factories send out a cheap or inferior article of doors, &c., put together from the machine, without being smoothed off, imperfectly framed together, and made out of half-seasoned lumber. This kind of work soon shrinks becomes loose and shaky, and racks to pieces, and has caused, in the minds of many persons, strong objections to all factory work.

This catalog is quite representative of others of the period, although some illustrated more selections of mouldings. A very large Ohio firm, for example, offered over 230 mouldings in 1862, and a Rome, New York, dealer illustrated 278 of them in 1873. Later in the century styles of mouldings, railings, and other items of interior finish were standardized by members of the Wholesale Sash, Door and Blind Manufacturers' Association of the Northwest and by the Eastern Sash, Door and Blind Manufacturers' Association, who adopted as well a uniform numbering system for the products. While the completeness of the Stevens catalog is otherwise impressive, one is struck by the conservative quality of the designs. Stevens was manufacturing doors in 1879, for instance, that had been offered by other firms at least twenty years earlier, and apparently was unaffected by the so-called Eastlake style that swept the country in the 1870's.

The author gratefully wishes to acknowledge the assistance provided by Paul R. Huey, Harley J. McKee, John I. Mesick, Jacquelyn M. Steck, Robert M. Vogel and John G. Waite.

Suggestions for Further Reading

CLARK, VICTOR S. *History of Manufactures in the United States 1860-1914*. Washington: Carnegie Institution of Washington, 1928.

CONDIT, CARL W. *American Building Art*. New York: Oxford University Press, 1961.

DAVEY, NORMAN. *A History of Building Materials*. London: Phoenix House, 1961.

Eighty Years' Progress of the United States. New York: L. Stebbins, 1861.

FITCH, JAMES MARSTON. *American Building, The Forces That Shape It*. Boston: Houghton Mifflin Co., 1972.

GIEDION, SIEGFRIED. *Mechanization Takes Command*. New York: W. W. Norton & Co., Inc., 1969.

GLOAG, JOHN, AND BRIDGWATER, DEREK. *A History of Cast Iron in Architecture*. London: George Allen and Unwin Ltd., 1948.

GREELEY, HORACE, ET AL. *The Great Industries of the United States*. Hartford: J. B. Burr & Hyde, 1872.

HITCHCOCK, HENRY-RUSSELL. *Architecture: Nineteenth and Twentieth Centuries*. Baltimore: Penguin Books, 1963.

Industrial Chicago. Vols. I and II: Chicago: The Goodspeed Pub. Co., 1891.

KOUWENHOVEN, JOHN A. *Made in America*. Garden City: Doubleday & Company, Inc., 1962.

LOSSING, BENSON J. *History of American Industries and Arts*. Philadelphia: Porter & Coates, 1878.

PETERSON, CHARLES E. "Iron in Early American Roofs," *The Smithsonian Journal of History*, Vol. 3 (1968), pp. 41–76.

MARSHALL LEFFERTS & BROTHER, 1854

When Marshall Lefferts died in 1876, he was honored chiefly for his service as a colonel with the Seventh Regiment of New York and little mention was made of his business career. He was, however, a leader in the American manufacture of galvanized iron and in the building of telegraph lines in this country.

Born in 1821, Lefferts received a public school education and later became engaged in engineering work in surveying Brooklyn. Shortly thereafter he entered the New York importing house of Morewood & Co. and soon became a partner. This firm was engaged extensively in importing zinc wire and other products used in the erection of telegraph lines. His experience in this firm led him to establish his own business under the name of Marshall Lefferts in 1852. One of his first activities during that year was to publish a catalog much like the 1854 one reproduced here, although the 1852 edition was not illustrated.

About this time Edmund Morewood was engaged in experiments with the manufacture of galvanized iron in England, being granted patents between 1841 and 1852, and it would not be surprising that he dealt with the New York firms. One of Morewood's patents was for coating iron with tin and zinc and Lefferts did carry "galvanized tinned iron" when he first established his firm. Edmund Morewood's patent, however, specified that the iron should be coated first with tin and then zinc, the reverse of Sorel's process mentioned in the introduction, but both techniques were designed to give the finished product a shinier appearance. Furthermore, Lefferts makes reference in Plate 3 of the 1854 catalog to "Morwood's Book," and, as a footnote, one of his five sons was named George Morewood Lefferts.

In 1849 Lefferts also became president of the New York, New England and New York State Telegraph Company and served until about 1860 when it was consolidated with other lines. Meanwhile in 1853 his brother, John A. Lefferts, entered the galvanizing business, and the company became known as Marshall Lefferts and Brother. This firm continued in business until 1861, not only handling imported products but also engaging in manufacture. In 1862 Marshall Lefferts briefly operated the business alone.

In 1861 he had become electrical engineer of the newly formed American Telegraph Company, which he turned into what was called "the most complete, efficient, and thoroughly organized telegraphic system in the world." During 1861-63 Lefferts served in the Civil War, and from 1869 until his death he was president of the Gold and Stock Telegraph Company. He summarized his interests in these fields thus in 1852: "We have certainly seen, within the last half century, the most surprising changes in the condition of human affairs, brought about by the scientific application of established principles to practical uses. . . . The progress of science has in nothing been more marked than in its use of electro-galvanism, to form such a combination of metals which shall completely neutralise this tendency of iron to rust."

Lefferts' entrance into the galvanized iron business coincided with the discovery and mining of zinc in this country. Mines had been opened in northern New Jersey in 1848 and in eastern Pennsylvania in 1853, but it was not until about 1860 that spelter, the metallic zinc needed for galvanizing, was successfully made in the United States from domestic zinc ores. Consequently the spelter initially used by Lefferts undoubtedly was imported from Europe, but in his work with the telegraph, he probably used American zinc, which was greatly preferred to the European.

Meanwhile in 1863 John C. Lefferts engaged in the galvanizing business, which became John C. Lefferts & Co. in 1865–66 when George M. Lefferts, Marshall Lefferts' son, joined the firm. In 1867 another son, Marshall Lefferts, Jr., replaced his brother in the company, and in 1873 he took over the business, which continued as Marshall Lefferts and Co. until 1909.

PATENT

GALVANIZED IRON,

BEING

PERFECTLY RUST PROOF,

THE CHEAPEST AND MOST

DURABLE MATERIAL

FOR

ROOFS, GUTTERS, SPOUTS, LEADERS, BATHING-TUBS,
TELEGRAPHIC WIRES, SHIPS' BOLTS, SPIKES,
FENCES, LIGHTNING RODS, ETC.

〜〜〜〜〜

IMPORTED AND MANUFACTURED BY

MARSHALL LEFFERTS & BROTHER,

70 & 71 BROAD STREET.

〜〜〜〜〜

NEW YORK:
WM. C. BRYANT & CO., PRINTERS, 41 NASSAU ST., COR. LIBERTY.

1854.

Fig. 5.

Plate 1.

Fig. 6. Fig. 7. Fig. 8.

Plate No. 1.

Figure 5 represents a boarded roof partly covered with plain galvanized iron sheets. For this mode of roofing, the thickness should be either 26 or 28 gauge, in sheets 24 inches wide, by 72 in length.

The following are some of the advantages which this metal possesses over other articles used for similar purposes:

Durability, strength, and lightness,—possessing the strength of iron with perfect protection from rust or decay, and being exceedingly light, 28 gauge weighing 12 ounces to the foot, while slate weighs from 5 lbs. to 12 lbs. The sheets are also less liable than slates to accidental disturbance, if laid on the roof as described below:

DIRECTIONS FOR FIXING.

Figures 6 and 8 show a transverse section of the wood rolls (half full size), and two methods of securing the sheets thereto on the vertical joint. The rolls are fastened to the roof at distances of 23 inches apart from centre to centre. The sheets are turned up 1¼ inches on each side, and fastened to the roll with galvanized iron nails, care being taken to place the nails in the position indicated on the drawing, and not on the top of the rolls.

Figure 7 shows the lap (half full size) to be made at the ends of the sheets, which makes good the longitudinal joints on the roof, without the use of solder.

For patterns of galvanized tinned iron gutters and ridge cap, &c., see plates 6 and 7.

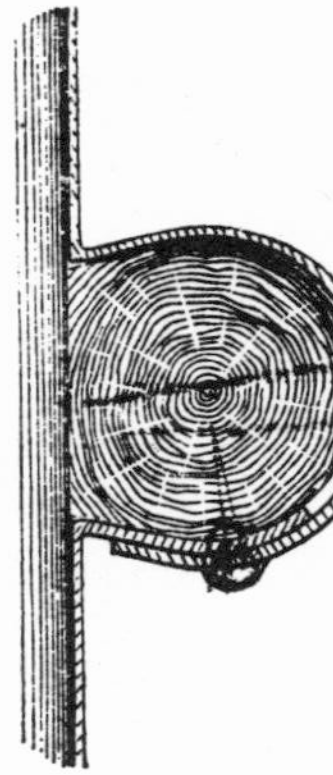

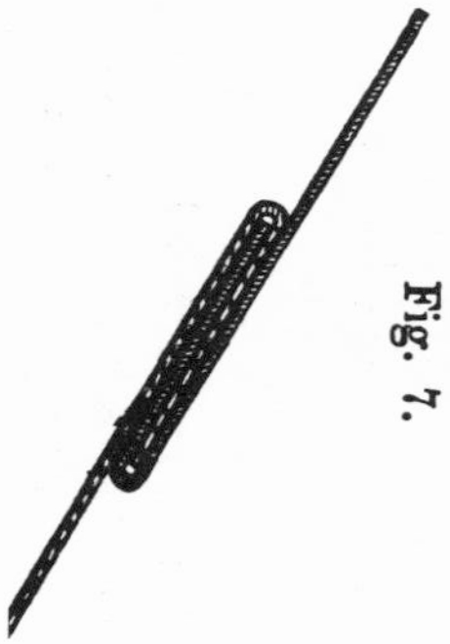

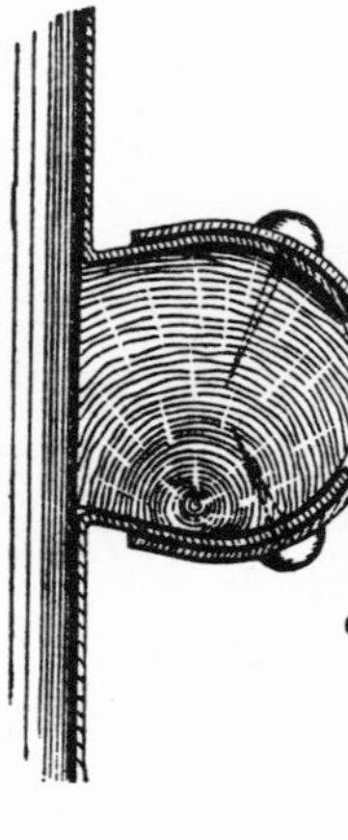

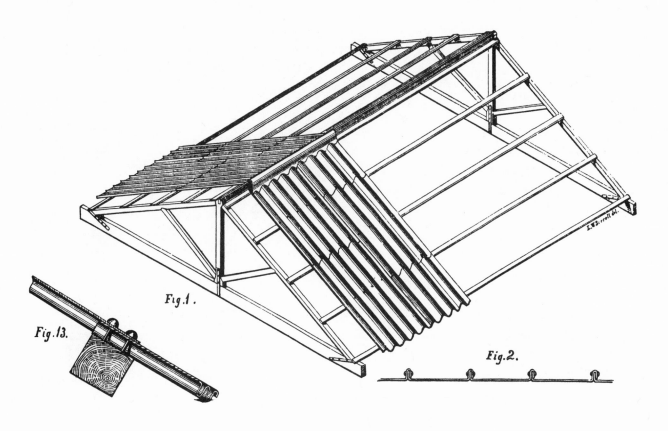

Fig. 1.

Fig. 13.

Fig. 2.

Plate No. 2.

The wooden frame work of a roof, 30 feet wide, partly covered with straight CORRUGATED GALVANIZED IRON. This form of sheet makes a very strong roof, and may be of either 18, 19, 20 or 22 guage iron.

The required strength for the rafters will depend entirely upon the size of the building, but as a guide, the frame work of the roof need not be over one-fourth as strong as would be necessary for slate, as a square of galvanized iron, 22 guage, weighs about 1¼ cwt., while a square of slate, of the usual kind, weighs from 10 to 12 cwt., and of the lightest kind from 7 to 8 cwt.

DIRECTIONS FOR FIXING.

The rafters about 8 feet apart, and the purlins 5 feet 8 inches apart from centre to centre.

Figure 1 shows the general arrangement of the corrugated sheets.

Figure 13 shows the iron fastened to the purlin, and the lap of the sheet, which should be 4 inches.

ANOTHER PLAN

As shewn on the opposite side of Plate 2, and transverse section, Fig. 2. But we would recommend in this case that the sheets be laid on boards, and 28 gauge Galvanized Iron used.

16

Plate .3

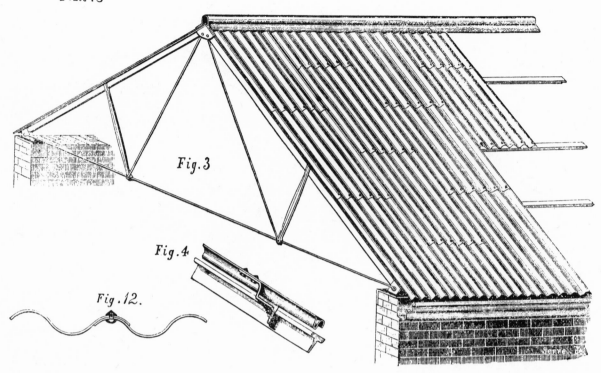

Fig. 3

Fig. 4

Fig. 12.

18

Plate No. 3.

Iron frame-work of a roof of 30 feet wide, partly covered with straight Corrugated Galvanized Iron. The rafters may be of either T, 3 × 3, or ⌐ iron; tie-rods ⅝ and ¾ inch, with light cast iron strut. The above may be varied according to the size of the building, but, as remarked for the preceding plan, Plate 2, need not be more than one-fourth as heavy in frame as would be required for slate covering.

DIRECTIONS.

Rafters are about 10 feet apart, or, if the purlins be trussed, then 12 to 15 feet apart.

Purlins 5 ft. 8 in. apart from centre to centre.

Fig. 4 shows a method of securing corrugated sheets to iron purlins, without riveting to the frame of the roof, thus allowing expansion and contraction, without disturbing the sheets.

Fig. 12 shows the side lap of the sheets, with rivet for fastening the sheets together.

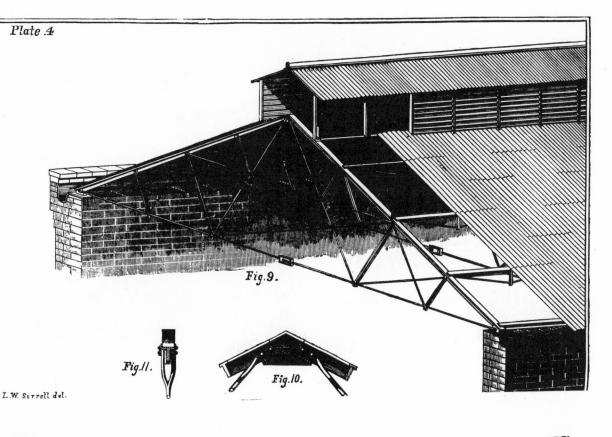

Fig. 9.

Fig. 11.

Fig. 10.

L.W. Serrell del.

20

Plate No. 4.

A Corrugated Galvanized Iron Roof, of large span, say 60 to 90 feet.

This description of roof is adapted to Railroad Depots, and manufacturing establishments, where a FIRE-PROOF and DURABLE ROOF is so essential. The weight of a square of this description of roof is about 500 lbs.; whilst a slate of square dimensions would be about 1500 lbs. A fact of sufficient importance to invite attention, even were none other to exist. But it must be borne in mind, that the SLATE ROOF is NOT FIRE-PROOF, and subject to more rapid decay. The magnificent railroad depots, which are to be found upon almost every line, are so substantially built, that, with a *fire-proof roof*, the companies can well become their OWN INSURERS, and thus save an immense amount of their present out lay.

FIG. 9 shows general plan; T rafters, cast-iron struts, round iron tie and tension rods.

PURLINS.—T iron, fifteen feet apart, and trussed.

FIG. 10.—Transversed section of rafter, at peak, showing method of fastening with tie rods.

FIG. 11.—Different view of No. 10.

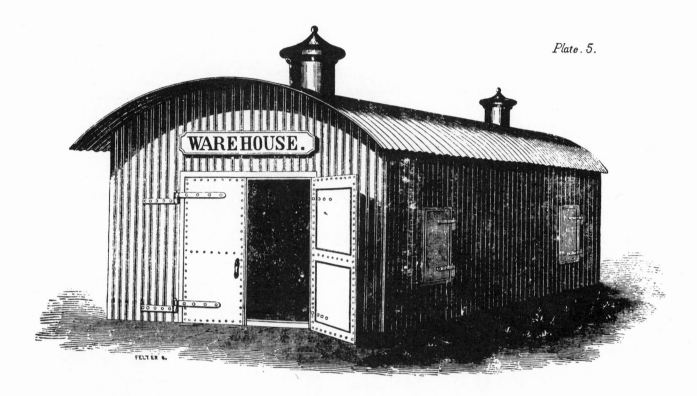

WAREHOUSE.

FELTER &.

Plate. 5.

24

Plate No. 5.

SHOWING CORRUGATED IRON WAREHOUSE.

This style of building is constructed of any length and of breadth up to 30 feet, and designed as a CHEAP and easy structure. They are just the thing for RAIL ROAD SHEDS, and may be finished with or without sides. No frame work is used except tie rods which are fastened to the flange on a cast iron gutter, to which the sheets are riveted.

Plate No. 6.

SLIP JOINT HALF ROUND GUTTER.

The wires d d fit into the bead a a, and c fits into the socket b, which is to be filled with red or white lead. No soldering is necessary.

The brackets for supporting the gutter should be galvanized.

Fig. 15—Stamped Eves' Gutter.

Fig. 14—Ridge Cap.

Plate No. 7.

STYLES OF GUTTERS MADE OF GALVANIZED IRON.

Fig. 16. Fig. 18.

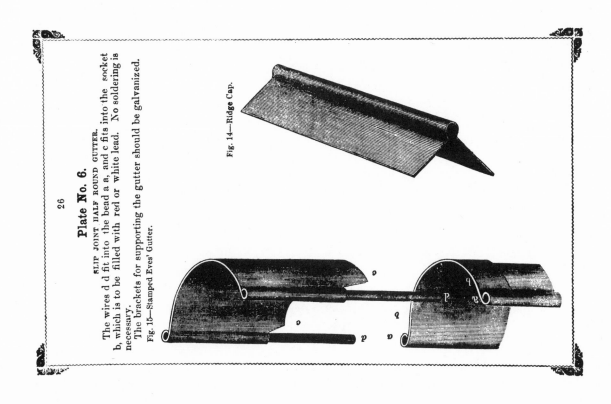

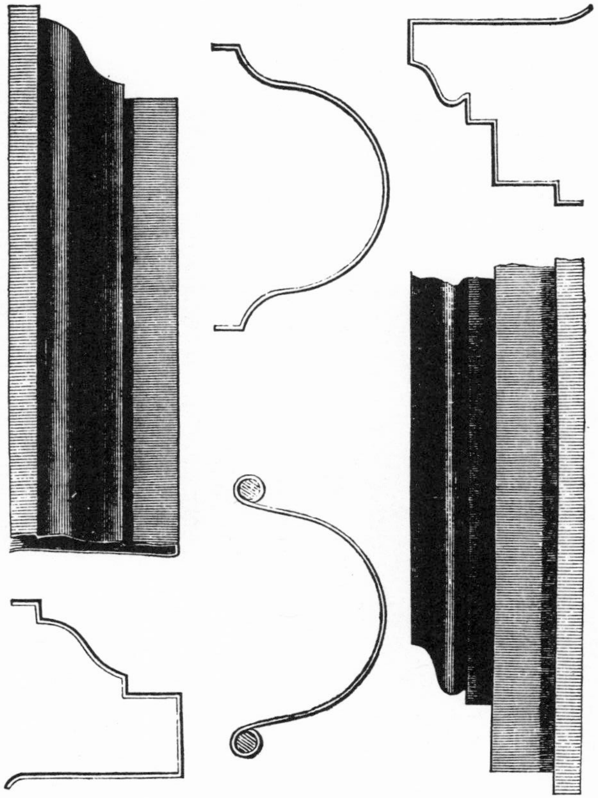

BUFFALO EAGLE IRON WORKS COMPANY, 1859

The Buffalo Eagle Iron Works Company was founded in 1853, during an era of "unbounded prosperity" that enveloped Buffalo as the western terminus of the Erie Canal. The resulting "mighty flow of commerce that rolled through the city" was in large measure due to the producers of the agricultural commodities of the west and northwest, which were being shipped to the eastern markets via the canal. It was to these "western friends" as well as to the builders of Buffalo that the Eagle Iron Works directed their catalogs of architectural iron products. Buffalo's population had increased from 2,412 at the opening of the canal era in 1825 to 29,773 in 1845 and, astonishingly, to 42,261 just five years later, thus creating an overwhelming demand for economical building materials that could be produced and assembled with great rapidity.

Assuming a name extraordinarily common in the iron industry, the Eagle Iron Works was established as a stock company with five partners, several of whom were also connected with the Eagle Furnace, an extensive stove foundry adjoining the iron works property in the heavily industrialized southern section of the city. In 1855 a writer described the installation during its first year of operation:

> This concern went into operation on the first of January, 1854, with a capital of $50,000. The foundry erected by the company is situated on the corner of Perry and Mississippi streets, and is 85 by 96 feet. The finishing shop is 60 by 90 feet, five stories high. Here are manufactured machinery and castings of every description. The value of the raw material consumed during the past season is $45,000—amount of work turned out $85,000. The average number of hands employed is about 100. The company possess facilities for doing a very large and profitable business.

At the outset of this first year of operation, the company also published a "Specimen Book" containing "Designs for Window Caps and Sills, Columns, etc.," in which the proprietors noted that they proposed "to pay particular attention to Architectural Iron Work."

Apparently the architectural casting business proved successful, for the introduction to the catalog of 1859 mentioned that others had been issued on an annual basis, commented that the firm was "continually adding to our stock of Patterns," which were too numerous to have all illustrated, and acknowledged the "liberal patronage of our friends." This introductory statement also suggested that these iron products continued to find a market both at home and "at a distance," for the proprietors invited customers "to call and see us before purchasing elsewhere," but also included a price list for the convenience of others.

While the types of components and several of the same designs were offered by the Eagle Iron Works in 1859 as in 1854, there were some remarkable differences. During this period two quite simple window cap styles were eliminated, while eighteen new styles (nos. 28 and 30–46 shown on pages 9–14) were added. Door cap designs underwent even more radical changes. In 1859 only one style (no. 52) remained of the initial offerings, three of which were very similar to window cap designs nos. 2, 5 and 10 shown on page 7 of the 1859 catalog, with the fourth having a fanlight beneath a fairly flat pointed arch; and five new door caps had been added by 1859. These changes reflected a growing demand for more heavily decorated and flamboyantly articulated building trim, as well as for arched openings, both segmental and stilted, all of which would have been expensive to execute in stone. Furthermore, by 1859 six new bracket styles (nos. 21–26) had been introduced, along with seven new pier and column designs (nos. 14 and 17–22). These designs had grown increasingly intricate since 1854, and one wonders about the nature of the other "designs only intended for ornament" that had been included in the catalogs published during the intervening years, but omitted in 1859.

In 1860 Robert Dunbar, initially a partner and the foundry superintendent, and S. W. Howell took over the business (which fact accounts for the annotated title page of the 1859 catalog), and immediately commenced work on alterations and additions to the foundry "necessitated by the advancement of the times." But they retained the same site, which was convenient for heavy industry. On the east the property was bounded by the Clark and Skinners Canal, which opened into the Buffalo River that in turn emptied into Lake Erie, and nearby was the New York, Lackawanna and Western Railroad.

About 1874 Howell left the firm to become a proprietor of the Niagara Mills, and in 1875 with the addition of George H. Dunbar, the firm became known as R. Dunbar and Son. During this period the works apparently expanded their production of the other items listed in the 1859 catalog, including steam engines, boilers, saw mills, hoisting machines, gears, and other industrial components. The firm specialized in the design and manufacture of grain elevator machinery, and the elder Dunbar received wide recognition for his designs of elevators. In 1877 the Eagle Iron Works advertised primarily as "General Machinists," not mentioning any architectural castings, but in 1891 immediately before R. H. Dunbar's death, the firm prominently advertised architectural iron work, although the specific items were not mentioned. George H. Dunbar continued to operate the works through 1898, but in 1899 he was listed in the city directory as a grain elevator architect and beginning in 1900 as vice-president of the Paragon Wall Plaster Company. In 1901 the Eagle Iron Works was in operation again, but under new ownership, manufacturing ice-making and refrigerating machinery.

This diversification of manufacture was probably a result not only of R. H. Dunbar's very successful response to Buffalo's phenomenal growth as a grain center but also of the slackening in the demand for cast iron building components resulting from the general distrust in the performance of unprotected iron during fire and from competition from sheet metal and machine-carved stone trim. Another factor may have been the difficulties involved in managing two quite separate foundry operations—for heavy (machinery) and light (architectural) castings—which involved different types of materials and labor, on a comparatively small, restricted site.

Buffalo Eagle Iron Works Co.

CATALOGUE

OF

Architectural Designs

Dunbar & Howell

OFFICE AND WORKS,

CORNER OF PERRY AND MISSISSIPPI STREETS, BUFFALO, N. Y.

BUFFALO,
CLAPP, MATTHEWS & CO'S STEAM PRINTING HOUSE.
Office of the Morning Express.
1859.

TO THE PUBLIC.

THE BUFFALO EAGLE IRON WORKS .
BUFFALO, FEBRUARY, 1859.

We take pleasure in again waiting upon our customers with our Annual Catalogue of ARCHITECTURAL DESIGNS. We are continually adding to our stock of Patterns, so much so indeed, that we cannot undertake to exhibit them all in our Catalogue. We have this year taken from our book some of the designs only intended for ornament, confining our exhibition to such articles as are wanted for general use.

Our HOISTING WHEELS are much used for stores and warehouses. We make them with Double and Single Gear, to hoist heavy and light weights. The price will be found lower than heretofore.

We venture to issue a price list for our CAPS AND SILLS FOR WINDOWS AND DOORS, thinking it will be found convenient by our friends at a distance. The price, it will be understood includes a coat of paint, all extras and cartages. *Our prices shall be as low as the lowest, and our work as good as the best.*

Our assortment of patterns for STORE FRONTS is very large and of great variety, both fancy and plain, heavy and light. We can suit any and all, as to style and cost. We continue to make the Rolling Iron Shutters for Store Fronts.

Thankful for the liberal patronage our friends have heretofore extended to us, we hope by our large assortment of Patterns, prompt and correct execution of orders, to make it for the interest of purchasers to call and see us before purchasing elsewhere.

Dunbar & Howell
Proprietors

ROBERT DUNBAR, *Supt.*

N. B.—We call attention to a partial list of articles made at this establishment, which may be found at the back end of this book.

PRICE LIST OF ARCHITECTURAL IRON WORK.

WINDOW AND DOOR CAPS.

Style No.	Opening in Wall Ft. In.	Opening of Cap Ft. In.	Price $ Ct.
1	3 0	Same.	4 50
1	3 3	do	5 00
1	3 4	do	5 50
1	3 6	do	6 00
2	3 0	do	6 25
2	3 2	do	6 25
2	3 3	do	6 50
2	3 4	do	6 50
2	3 6	do	6 75
2	4 0	do	7 00
3	3 0	do	4 00
3	3 3	do	4 50
3	3 4	do	5 00
3	3 6	do	5 50
4	3 2	do	3 00
4	3 4	do	3 25
5	3 0	do	3 00
5	3 3	do	3 25
5	3 4	do	3 50
5	3 6	do	3 75
5	3 7	do	4 00
5	3 9	do	4 25
5	4 0	do	4 50
5	5 0	do	6 50
5	5 6	do	7 00
5	6 0	do	7 50
5	6 5	do	8 00
7	2 6	do	2 50
7	3 0	do	2 75
7	3 3	do	3 00
7	3 6	do	3 25
7	3 9	do	3 75
7	4 0	do	4 25
7	5 0	do	5 50
9	3 3	do	3 00
9	3 6	do	3 50
10	2 6	do	3 00
10	3 0	do	3 50
10	3 3	do	3 50
10	3 5	do	4 00
10	3 6	do	4 00
10	3 8	do	4 00
10	4 7	do	5 00
10	5 0	do	5 75
10	5 6	do	6 50
10	6 0	do	....
11	3 0	do	10 00
11	3 2	do	11 00
11	4 0	do	....

Style No.	Opening in Wall Ft. In.	Opening of Cap Ft. In.	Price $ Ct.
12	3 0	Same.	9 00
12	3 3	do	10 00
12	3 4	do	10 00
12	4 0	do	11 00
12	4 4	do	11 00
12	6 8	do	....
13	3 3	do	....
13	3 4	do	3 75
13	3 8	do	....
13	4 0	do	4 25
14	2 10	do	4 00
14	3 0	3 4	....
14	3 4	3 8	....
15	3 6	Same.	....
15	4 0	do	....
17	2 6	do	2 75
17	3 0	do	3 00
17	3 3	do	3 25
17	3 6	do	3 50
17	3 9	do	4 00
17	4 0	do	4 50
18	3 1	do	6 00
18	3 3	do	6 50
18	3 4	do	6 75
18	3 6	do	7 50
18	3 8	do	7 50
19	2 6	do	3 50
19	3 0	do	4 00
19	3 3	do	4 00
19	3 4	do	4 75
19	3 5	do	4 50
19	3 6	do	4 50
19	3 7	do	4 50
19	5 0	do	5 50
19	5 6	do	6 25
19	6 0	do	7 00
22	2 0	do	6 50
22	2 7	do	7 00
22	3 4	do	9 00
22	4 0	do	....
22	4 3	do	....
22	4 6	do	....
23	3 2	do	....
23	4 0	do	....
23	5 6	do	....
26	3 4	do	5 25
26	3 6	do	5 50
..	. .	do	....

Style No.		Opening in Wall Ft. In.	Opening of Cap Ft. In.	Price $ Ct.
27		3 2	Same.	12 00
28		2 0	do	6 00
28		2 7	do	6 50
28		3 4	do	8 00
28		4 0	do	....
28		4 3	do	....
28		4 6	do	....
30		3 6	do	8 50
30		4 0	do	9 50
31	Without Keystone	3 0	3 4	6 00
		3 2	3 6	6 25
		3 3	3 7	6 50
		3 4	3 8	6 75
		3 6	3 10	7 00
		5 3	5 7	....
		6 0	6 4	....
31	With Keystone	3 0	3 4	6 50
		3 2	3 6	6 75
		3 3	3 7	7 00
		3 4	3 8	7 25
		3 6	3 10	7 50
		5 3	5 7	....
		6 0	6 4	....
32	With Vace, &c	3 0	3 4	16 00
		3 2	3 6	16 50
		3 4	3 8	17 25
		3 6	3 10	18 00
		3 11	3 11	....
		6 0	6 5	....
32	With Middle Ornament	3 0	3 4	11 00
		3 2	3 6	11 50
		3 4	3 8	12 25
		3 6	3 10	13 00
		3 11	3 11	....
		6 0	6 5	....
33		3 11	3 11	40 00
34		7 to 9ft.	With 2 to 4 Brackets	....
35	With Top Orna-m'nts	3 6	Same.	15 00
		3 10	do	16 00
		3 11	do	16 50
35	W'out Top Orna-m'nts	3 6	do	10 00
		3 10	do	10 50
		3 11	do	11 00
36		3 2	3 6	11 00
36		4 0	4 4	11 50
36		4 4	4 8	12 00

PRICE LIST OF ARCHITECTURAL IRON WORK.

WINDOW AND DOOR CAPS.

Style No.	Opening in Wall Ft.	In.	Opening of Cap Ft.	In.	Price $ Ct.
36	5	2	5	6	....
36	5	6	5	10	....
37	3	0	3	4	7 50
37	3	2	3	6	7 75
37	3	3	3	7	8 00
37	3	4	3	8	8 25
37	3	6	3	10	8 50
37	5	3	5	7	....
37	6	0	6	4	....
38	3	0	3	4	13 50
38	3	2	3	6	14 00
38	3	4	3	8	14 75
38	3	6	3	10	15 50
38	3	11	3	11	....
39	3	0	3	4	8 50
39	3	2	3	6	8 75
39	3	3	3	7	9 00
39	3	4	3	8	9 25
39	3	6	3	10	9 50
39	5	3	5	7	....
39	6	0	6	4	....
40	6	4	6	8	....
41	4	4	4	8	....
41	5	0	5	4	....

Style No	Opening in Wall Ft.	In.	Opening of Cap Ft. In.	Price $ Ct.
41	6	4	6 8	....
42	4	0	Same.	13 00
42	4	4	do	14 50
42	5	0	do	16 00
42	6	4	do	23 00
43	3	0	do	7 00
43	3	2	do	7 00
43	3	3	do	7 25
43	3	4	do	7 25
43	3	6	do	7 50
43	4	0	do	8 50
43	5	6	do	9 00
43	5	9	do	9 50
43	6	0	do	....
44	2	6	do	4 25
44	3	0	do	4 50
44	3	3	do	4 75
44	3	5	do	5 00
44	3	6	do	5 25
44	3	7	do	5 50
44	5	0	do	9 00
44	5	6	do	9 75
44	6	0	do	10 50
45	3	0	do	4 50

Style No.	Opening in Wall Ft In	Opening of Cap Ft In	Price $ Ct.
45	3 3	Same.	4 50
45	3 4	do	4 50
45	3 6	do	4 75
45	3 7	do	5 00
45	3 9	do	5 25
45	4 0	do	5 50
46	2 6	do	4 00
46	3 0	do	4 25
46	3 3	do	4 50
46	3 6	do	4 75
46	3 8	do	5 00
46	3 9	do	5 25
46	4 0	do	5 50
47	4 10	do	....
48	2 9	do	....
48	4 6	do	....
49	5 10	do	....
49	6 7	do	....
50	Each Ope'g 3½ feet, Total, 7½ f.	do	....
51	4 1	do	....
51	5 2	do	....
52	4 6	do	4 50

WINDOW SILLS.

MADE ANY DESIRED OPENING.

Style No.	Opening in Wall Ft.	In.	Price $ Ct.	Style No	Opening in Wall Ft.	In.	Price $ Ct.	Style No.	Opening in Wall Ft.	In	Price $ Ct.
1	3	0	2 75	6	3	0	2 00	11	3	6	4 50
1	3	3	3 00	6	3	3	2 25	11	4	0	5 00
1	3	4	3 00	6	3	4	2 25	..	.	.	....
1	3	6	3 25	6	3	6	2 50	..	.	.	....
1	3	9	3 50	6	3	9	2 50	..	.	.	....
1	4	0	3 50	6	4	0	2 75	..	.	.	....
2	3	1	2 50	7	3	0	3 25	..	.	.	....
2	3	3	2 75	7	3	4	3 50	..	.	.	....
2	3	4	2 75	7	4	0	3 75	..	.	.	....
2	3	6	3 00					..	.	.	....
2	3	8	3 25	8	2	7	3 00	..	.	.	....
2	4	0	3 25	8	3	4	3 25	..	.	.	....
3	4	4	4 25	9	3	0	2 00	..	.	.	....
				9	3	3	2 25	..	.	.	....
4	3	11	12 00	9	3	6	2 50	..	.	.	....
5	3	2	2 25	10	3	6	3 50	..	.	.	....
5	3	6	2 50	10	4	0	4 00	..	.	.	....

BRACKETS AND CONSOLES.

Style No.	Projection Ft.	In.	Face Ft.	In.	Price $ Ct
5	2	3	.	.	....
13	1	3	.	6	....
19	.	6½	.	9	2 00
21	2	8	.	8	7 50
22	1	7	.	8	3 75
22	1	0	.	6	2 50
23	.	10	.	5	1 25
23	.	9	.	5	1 00
23	.	7½	.	3¾	75
23	.	7	.	3¼	65
24	2	9	.	8	15 00
25	2	9	.	6	12 00
26	2	6	.	8	12 00

Architectural Designs.

WINDOW CAPS.

See Price List, Pages 4 & 5.

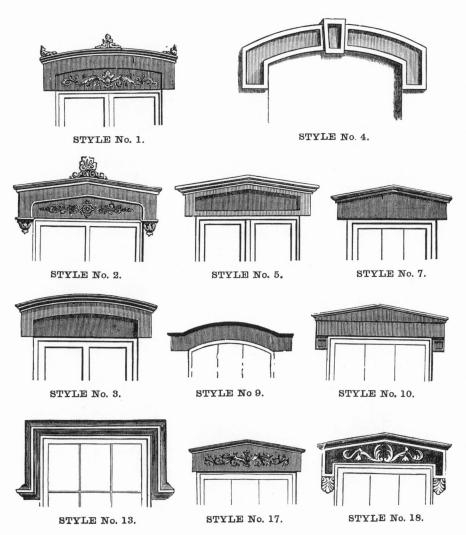

STYLE No. 1. STYLE No. 4.

STYLE No. 2. STYLE No. 5. STYLE No. 7.

STYLE No. 3. STYLE No 9. STYLE No. 10.

STYLE No. 13. STYLE No. 17. STYLE No. 18.

STYLE No. 15.

STYLE No. 19.

STYLE No. 26.

STYLE No. 11.   Scale 5-8.

STYLE No. 12.   Scale 5-8.

STYLE No. 23.

STYLE No. 33.   Scale 1-2.

STYLE No. 34.   Scale 5-16.

STYLE No. 40.   Scale 3-8.

STYLE No. 41.   Scale 1-2.

STYLE No. 43.   Scale 1-2.

STYLE No. 44.   Scale 3-8.

STYLE No. 45.   Scale 3-8.

STYLE No. 46.   Scale 3-8.

STYLE No. 14.

STYLE No. 24

STYLE No. 25.

STYLE No. 28.

STYLE No. 32.   Scale 3-8.

STYLE No. 20.

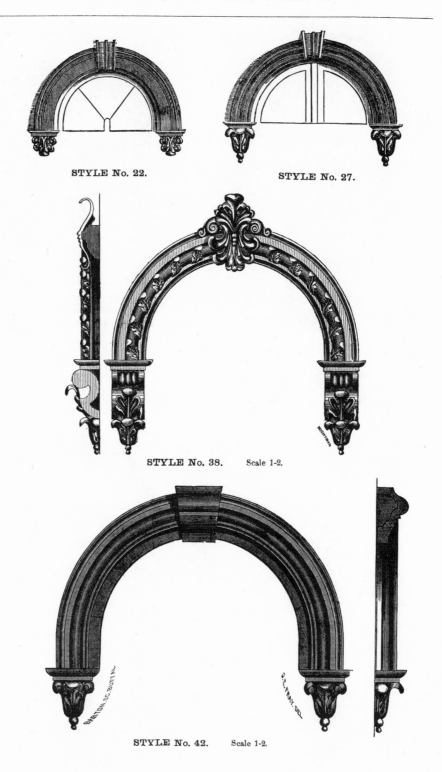

STYLE No. 22.   STYLE No. 27.

STYLE No. 38.   Scale 1-2.

STYLE No. 42.   Scale 1-2.

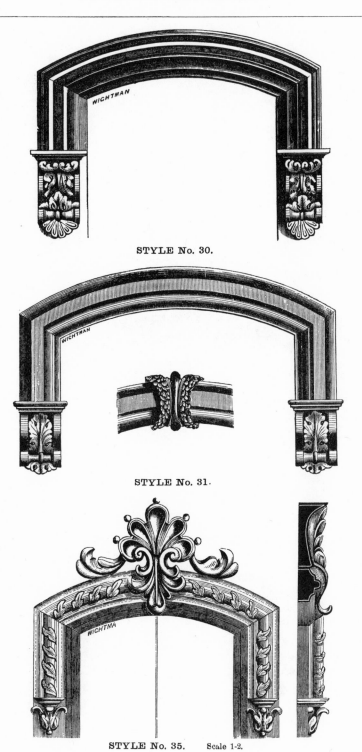

STYLE No. 30.

STYLE No. 31.

STYLE No. 35.   Scale 1-2.

STYLE No. 36.   Scale 1-2.

STYLE No. 37.   Scale 1-2.

STYLE No. 39.   Scale 1-2.

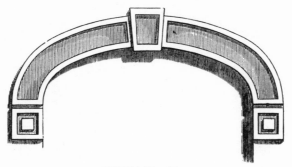

STYLE No. 52.

DOOR CAPS.

STYLE No. 47.   Scale 3-8.

STYLE No. 48.   Scale 1-2.

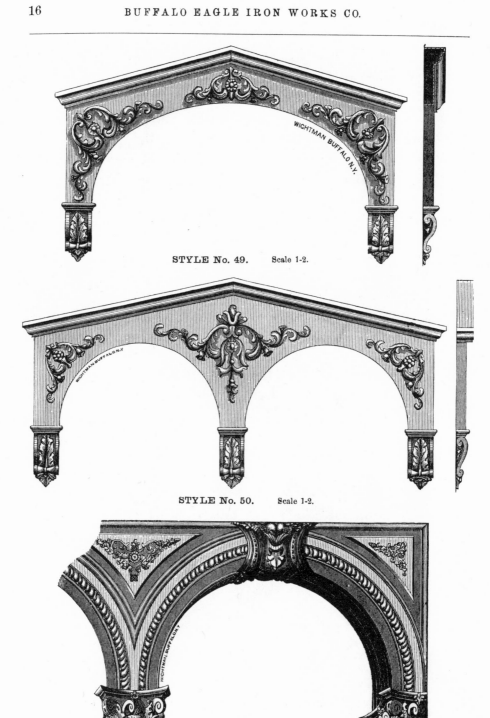

STYLE No. 49.   Scale 1-2.

STYLE No. 50.   Scale 1-2.

STYLE No. 51.   Scale 1-2.

ARCHES FOR STORE FRONTS.

STYLE No. 1.

For 3 feet 0 inch. opening.
do 4 do 5 do   do
do 4 do 0 do   do

STYLE No. 2.

For 5 feet 2 inch. opening.
do 5 do 6¼ do   do

STYLE No. 4.

For 6 feet 7¼ inch. opening.

WINDOW SILLS.

Made for any Opening desired.   See Price List, Page 5.

STYLE No. 1.

STYLE No. 2.

STYLE No. 3.

STYLE No. 4.

STYLE No. 5.

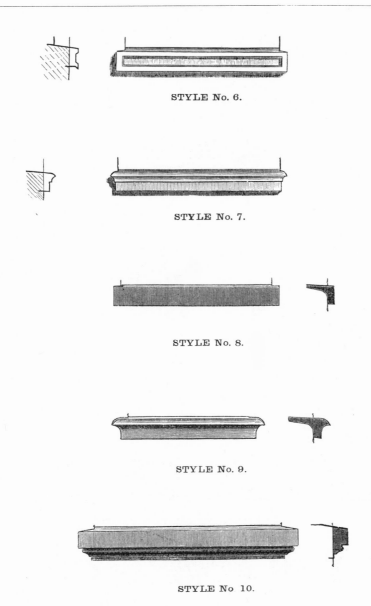

STYLE No. 6.

STYLE No. 7.

STYLE No. 8.

STYLE No. 9.

STYLE No 10.

STYLE No. 11.

BRACKETS AND ANTI-HEADS.

See Price List, Page 5.

STYLE No 5.

STYLE No. 13.

STYLE No. 14.

STYLE No. 21.   Scale 3-8.

STYLE No. 22.

STYLE No. 23.

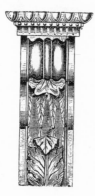
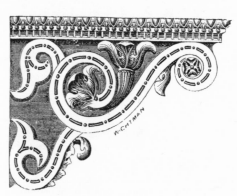

STYLE No. 24.   Scale 7-8.

STYLE No. 25.   Scale 7-8.

STYLE No. 26.   Scale 7-8.

ANTI-HEAD STYLE No. 4.

COLUMN HEADS.

STYLE No. 15.

STYLE No. 16.

STYLE No. 17.

STYLE No. 18.

BRACKET STYLE No. 17.

COLUMNS AND STORE FRONTS.

Made any Desired Length.

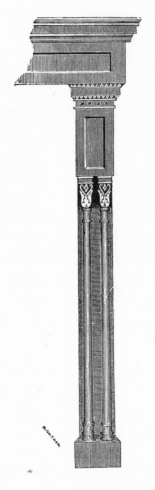

STYLE No. 1.

FRONT VIEW.

12 inch. face.

10 inch. deep.

FRONT VIEW.

6 inch. face.

10 inch. deep.

Made any Desired Length.

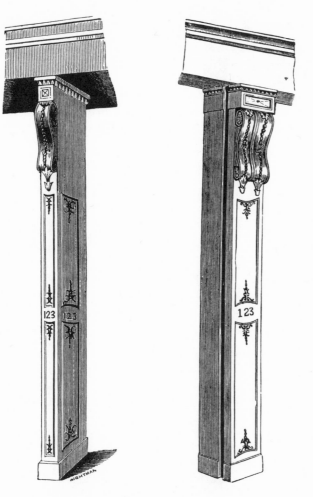

STYLE No. 3.

FRONT AND SIDE VIEW.	FRONT AND WINDOW SIDE VIEW.
4 inch. face.	10 inch. face.
10 do deep.	10 do deep.

STYLE No. 5.

4½ inch. diam. at neck.

6 do do do

7½ do do do

Pilasters for 8, 12, 16 inch wall, with side returns 2 to 10 inches deep.

Made any Desired Length.

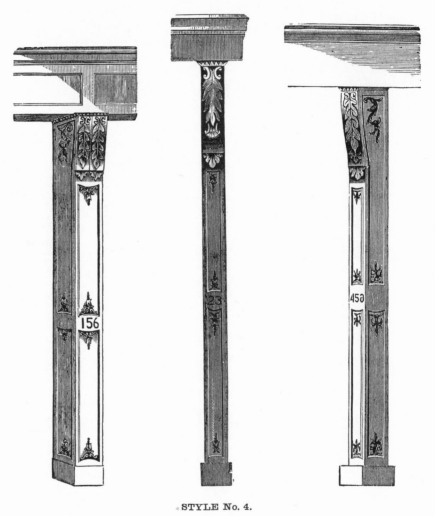

STYLE No. 4.

FRONT AND SIDE VIEW.	FRONT VIEW.	FRONT AND SIDE VIEW.
12 inch. face.	4 inch. face.	4 inch. face.
6 do deep.	6 do deep.	6 do deep.

Pilasters for 8, 12, 16 inch wall, with side returns from 2 to 6 inches deep.

Made any Desired Length.

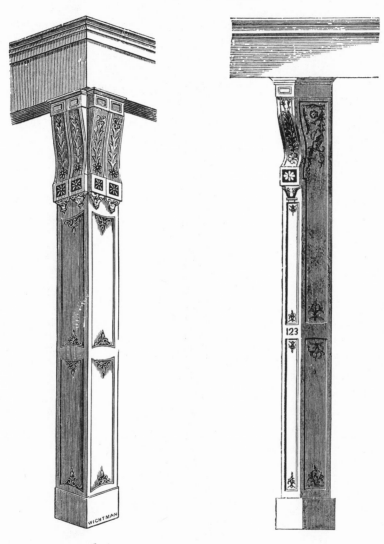

STYLE No. 7.

CORNER VIEW.   FRONT AND SIDE VIEW.

12 inch. both faces.   6 inch. face.
                                10 do deep.

Pilasters 12 and 16 inch walls, with side returns 2 to 10 inches deep.

Made any Desired Length.

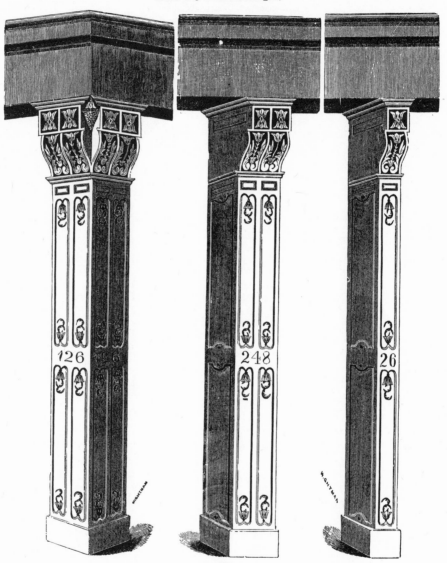

STYLE No. 9.

CORNER VIEW.　　　FRONT AND SIDE VIEW.　　　FRONT AND SIDE VIEW.

10 inch. both faces.　　　10 inch. face.　　　5 inch. face.
　　　　　　　　　　　10　do　deep.　　　10　do　deep.

Pilasters with side returns.

Made any Desired Length.

STYLE No. 6.

FRONT AND SIDE VIEW.   FRONT AND SIDE VIEW.

4 inch. face.   12 inch. face.

6, 8, 10 do. deep.   6, 8, 10 do deep.

STYLE No. 8.

FRONT VIEW—OCTAGON FACE.

Pilasters for 8 to 12 inch walls, with side returns 2 to 6 inches deep.

Made any Desired Length.

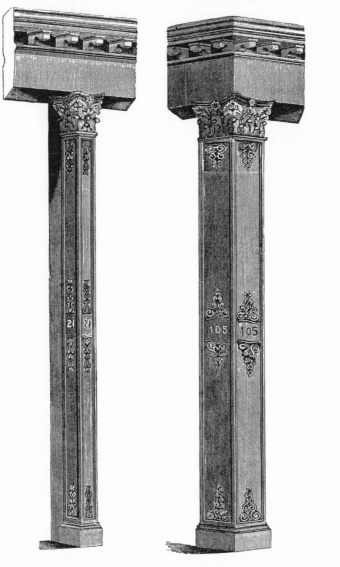

STYLE No. 10.   STYLE No. 11.

6 inch. face.   12 inch. face.   4½ inch. diameter.

12 and 14 do deep.   12 do deep.   5½ do   do

Pilasters from 6 to 16 inches return.   6 do   do

Made any Desired Length.

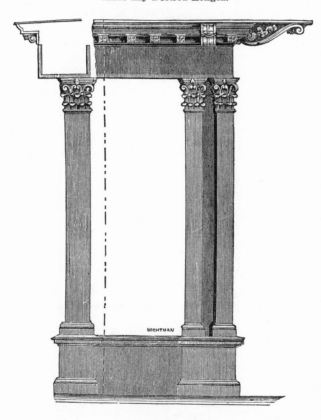

STYLE No. 13.

END VIEW.   FRONT VIEW AND CORNER.

12 inch. face, 24 inch. deep.   24 inch. face.
 5   do   do   8 to 10 inch. deep   24   do   deep.
with panel in column.

Made any Desired Length.

STYLE No. 14.

5 inch. face.

8, 10, 12 inch. deep.

Pilasters for 2 to 12 inch returns.

Made any Desired Length.

STYLE No. 15.

8, 12, and 16 inch. face.
12 and 16 inch. deep.

Made any Desired Length.

STYLE No. 16.

FRONT VIEW.	FRONT VIEW.
10 inch. face.	5 inch. face.
10 inch. deep.	10 inch. deep.

Pilasters return 2 to 12 inches.

Made any Desired Length.

STYLE No. 17.   Scale 3-S.

Made any Desired Length.

STYLE No. 22.   Scale 3-8.

Made any Desired Length.

STYLE No. 12.

Corinthian Column.

7 inch. diam. at neck.

8 do   do   do

9 do   do   do

12 do   do   do

STYLE No. 18.

Scale 3-8.

STYLE No. 19.

Scale 1.2.

STYLE No. 20.

Scale 3-8.

STYLE No. 21.

Scale 3-8.

GRATING TO GO UNDER WINDOW.

Either of these Patterns can be made of any size. Distance from centre to centre of circles, in each, is six inches.

MORRIS, TASKER & CO., 1860

Of the six companies represented in this book, Morris, Tasker & Co. was by far the largest in scale, being the "most extensive manufacturing establishment in the southern part of Philadelphia and the largest of its class in the country." The extent of their operations at the Pascal Iron Works was described in 1872:

> The *Pascal Iron Works* comprise twelve acres, covering two entire squares in Philadelphia, bounded by Third and Fifth streets in one direction, and by Morris and Tasker streets in another. They have also a large edifice on the opposite side of Morris street. . . .
>
> . . . The works, in 1872, constantly employed twelve boilers and seven steam engines, representing an aggregate of 1,000 horse-power. In the pipe mills might be seen a great number of furnaces for heating bent pipes preparatory to welding them in the smiths' shops; and in the machine shops were an almost endless variety of machine-tools for special purposes, representing the best makers.
>
> All the machinery of the establishment was in duplicate, to meet any emergency which might arise from breakage or other causes; so that it was hardly possible that any disaster could occur to cause the suspension of the work in the establishment for more than twenty-four hours. Most of the buildings were thoroughly fire-proof, and connected with the machinery was apparatus for the quick extinguishment of fire in any part of the buildings.
>
> The establishment afforded employment to about 1,600 persons. Only two-thirds of these were engaged during the day, and they were relieved by fresh relays at evening, the pipe-mills being kept constantly in operation day and night.

Another writer reported in 1867 that "the machinery is of the most approved description, much of it original with the firm, and surpasses, it is said, any that can be found in any similar establishment in England. Over forty thousand tons of anthracite coal are annually consumed in these works."

Philadelphia was at this time one of the country's leading iron centers, so it is not surprising that two catalogs of iron products in this collection were published by Philadelphia firms. The reasons for the city's prominence were explained in a discussion of Philadelphia manufacturers in 1858:

> It is probable that in no branch of the general manufactures of Philadelphia, is her superiority so widely known and generally conceded as in the fabrication of Metals. The abundance of Iron produced in the vicinity of the city, and its consequent cheapness, have naturally concentrated attention upon its manufactures, as well as extended its uses; while the fame of our Engineers and Machinists attracts from abroad a large and constantly increasing patronage.

Morris, Tasker & Co. had its beginnings in 1821 when Stephen P. Morris began casting stoves and grates. In 1835 Henry Morris and Thomas T. Tasker entered the business, which then became known as S. P. Morris & Co., which during the following year began manufacturing gas pipes. After S. P. Morris retired and Wistar Morris entered the firm, it became known as Morris, Tasker & Morris, but was changed in 1856 to Morris, Tasker & Co. In 1872–73 after several years of negotiations with the Philadelphia city government for permission to lay railroad tracks in the streets for their accommodation, the company purchased a large tract of land in New Castle, Del., and established an extensive iron works there. They also had branch offices in New York and Boston and made the cast iron work for the Main Exhibition Building at the Centennial Exposition of 1876. The firm continued to be listed in the Philadelphia directories until 1900.

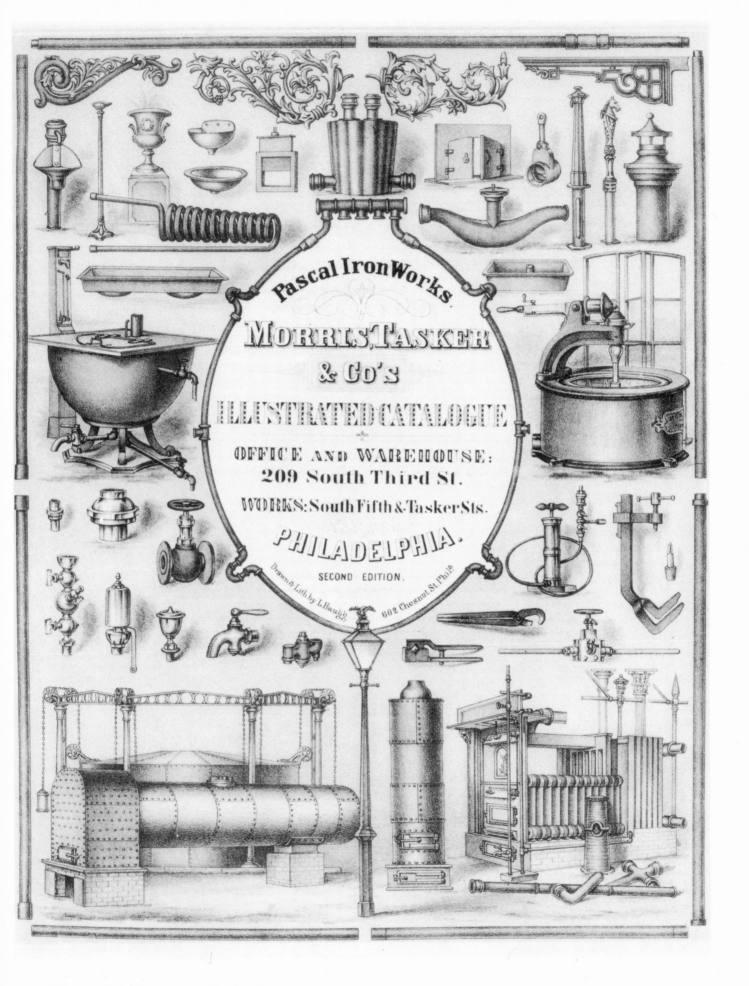

Pascal Iron Works.

MORRIS, TASKER & Co's

ILLUSTRATED CATALOGUE

OFFICE AND WAREHOUSE:
209 South Third St.

WORKS: South Fifth & Tasker Sts.

PHILADELPHIA.

SECOND EDITION.

Drawn & Lith. by L. Haugg 602 Chesnut St. Phila.

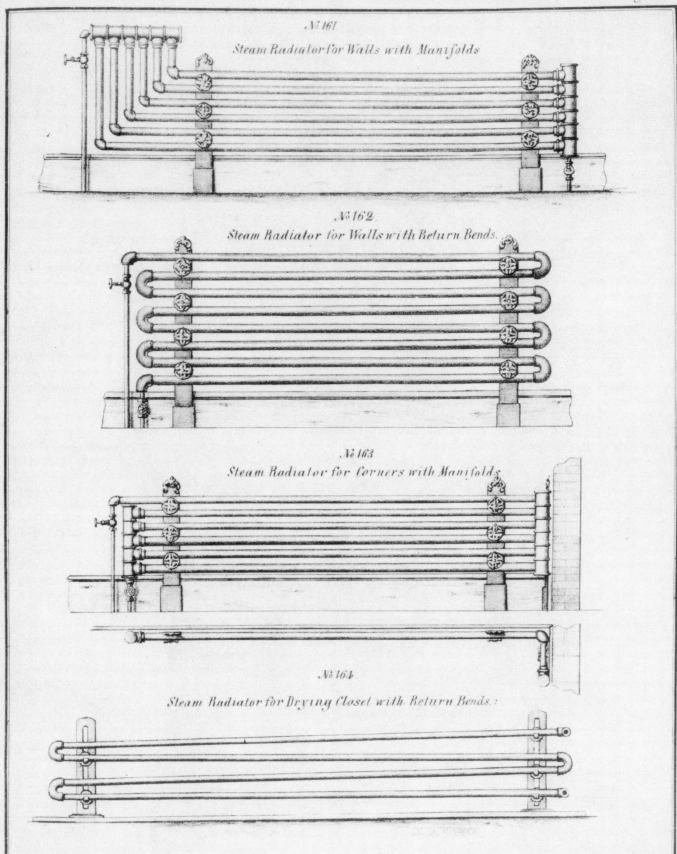

Nº 161.

Steam Radiator for Walls with Manifolds

Nº 162.

Steam Radiator for Walls with Return Bends.

Nº 163.

Steam Radiator for Corners with Manifolds

Nº 164.

Steam Radiator for Drying Closet with Return Bends.

Nº 183.
Ornamental Case for Steam Radiators.

Nº 184
Ornamental Case for Steam Radiators

N^o185.

Ventilator Fronts.

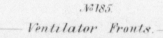

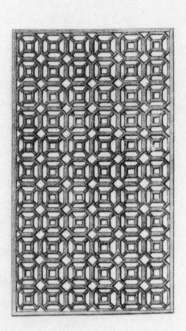

N^o186.

Backs & Jambs for Fire places.

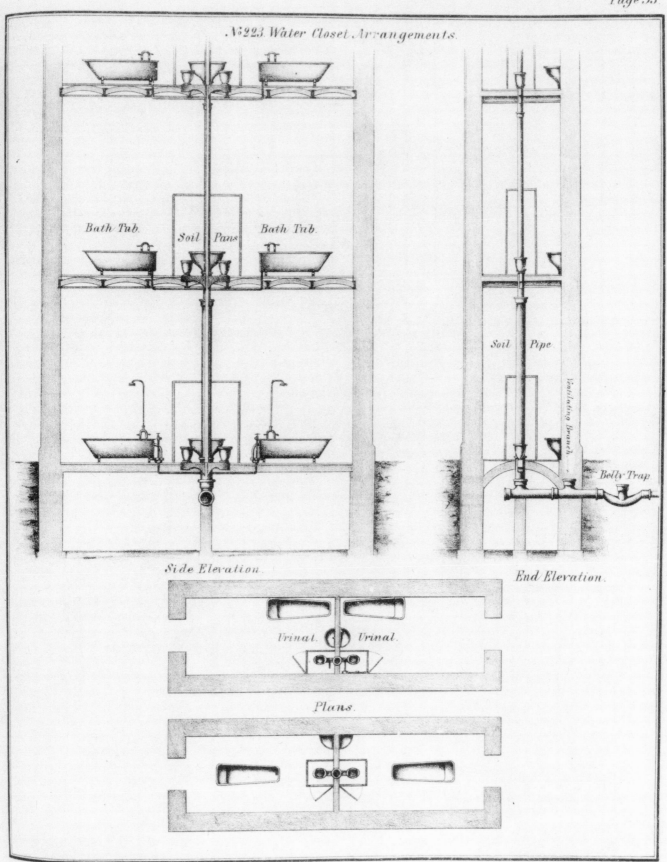

No 223. Water Closet Arrangements.

Bath Tub.   Soil   Pans   Bath Tub.

Soil   Pipe

Ventilating Branch.

Belly Trap.

Side Elevation.   End Elevation.

Urinal.   Urinal.

Plans.

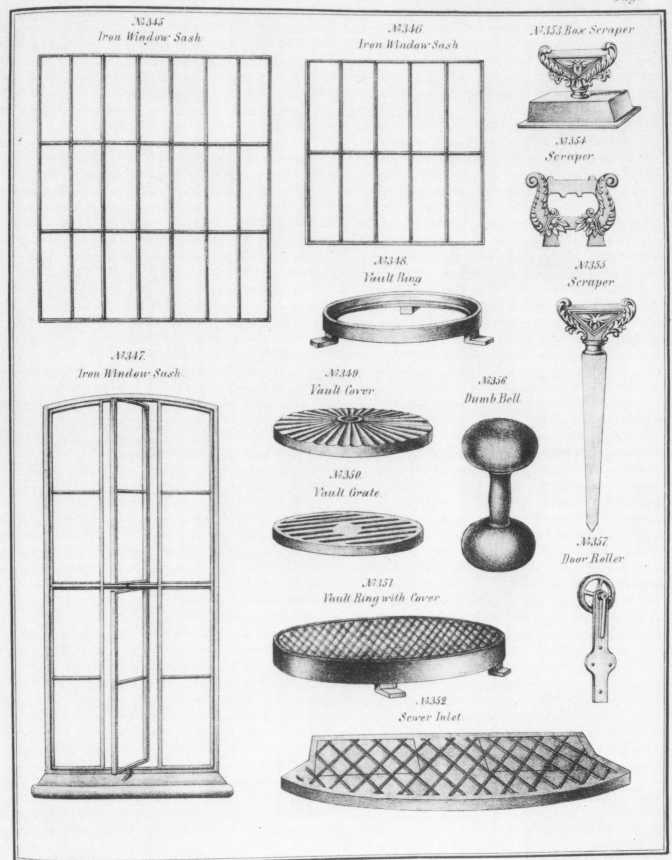

No. 345
Iron Window Sash

No. 346
Iron Window Sash

No. 353 Box Scraper

No. 354
Scraper

No. 348.
Vault Ring

No. 355
Scraper

No. 347.
Iron Window Sash

No. 349.
Vault Cover

No. 356.
Dumb Bell

No. 350.
Vault Grate

No. 357.
Door Roller

No. 351.
Vault Ring with Cover

No. 352.
Sewer Inlet.

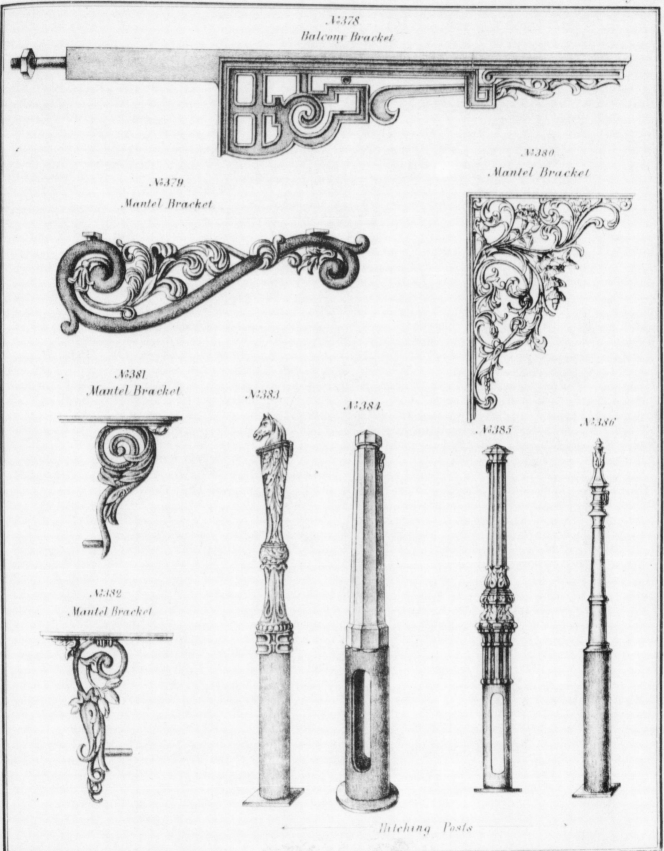

Nº 378
Balcony Bracket

Nº 380.
Mantel Bracket

Nº 379.
Mantel Bracket

Nº 381.
Mantel Bracket

Nº 383.

Nº 384.

Nº 385.

Nº 386.

Nº 382.
Mantel Bracket

Hitching Posts

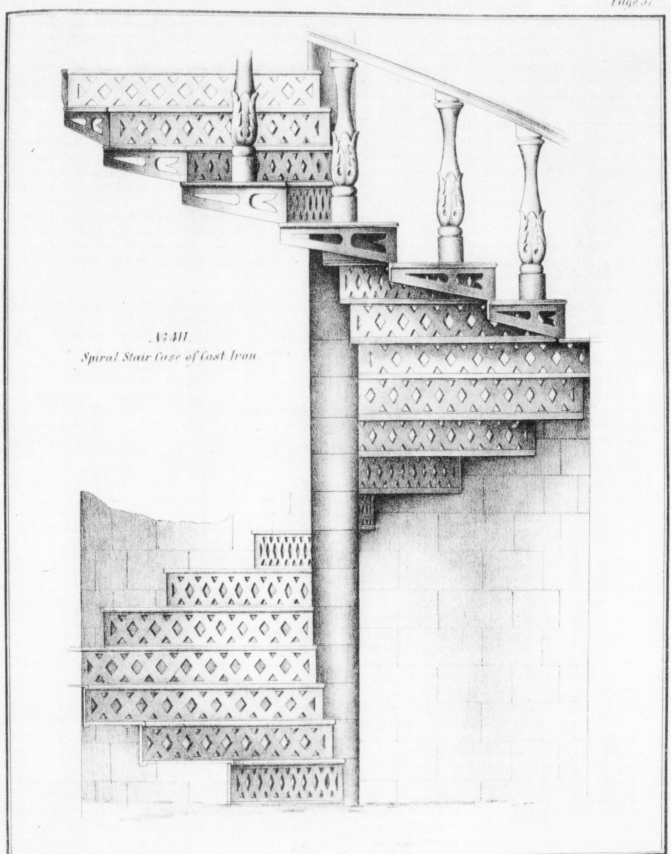

Nº 411.
Spiral Stair Case of Cast Iron.

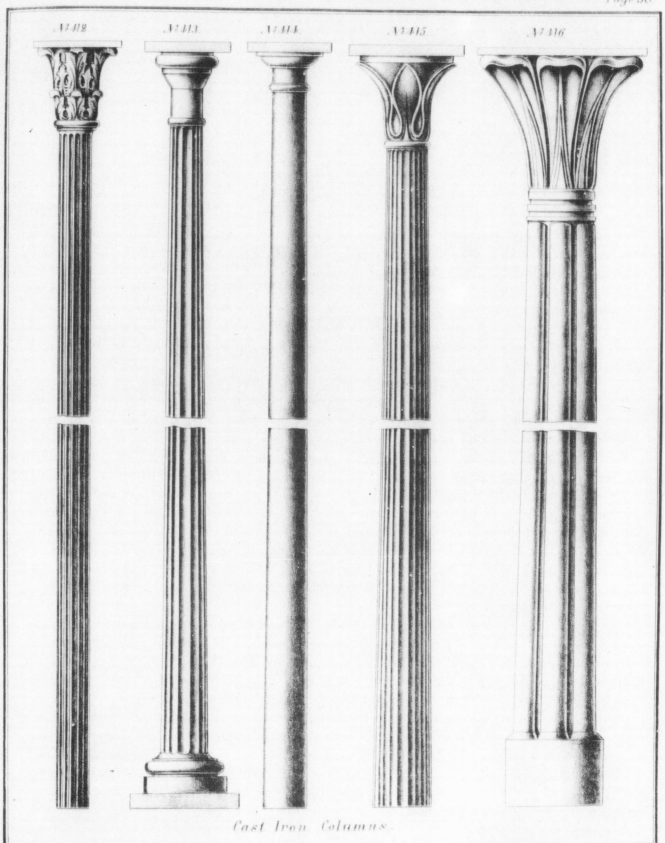

Cast Iron Columns.

PHILADELPHIA ARCHITECTURAL IRON CO., 1872

The Philadelphia Architectural Iron Company catalog was apparently issued shortly after the firm assumed its new name in 1872. Its predecessor, J. P. Stidham & Co., was first listed in the Philadelphia city directories in 1866 as an "iron roof manufacturer." Stidham, interestingly, was a physician, whose name appears in the directories during the 1850's, but without any indication that he was associated with an iron works. The 1872 catalog, however, states that the company was "one of the oldest in the country, having been established now fully 20 years, which gives us the benefit of a very extensive experience in our business," but there is no other information about its former name or location.

The Philadelphia Architectural Iron Company, whose partners were listed as Stidham, Jethro J. McCullough, and Delaplain M. Daniel, appeared in the directories through 1879. Stidham, though, had meanwhile joined the firm of Richards, Ingram & Co., metal refiners, located a few blocks north of the iron works. In 1880 he was listed simply as a physician.

The Architectural Iron Company was located at the corner of 11th Street and Washington Avenue in the south part of Philadelphia along with many other heavy industries. At the southeast corner of the same intersection the McCullough Iron Works had located their American Galvanizing Works. Reportedly the largest in the world, the McCullough plant also claimed to have introduced the manufacture of galvanized sheet iron to America in 1852, which, significantly, was the same year that Marshall Lefferts established his company in New York. The McCullough Iron Company also operated five rolling mills in Maryland where the iron plates were made. One wonders whether there was any connection with this firm and the Philadelphia Architectural Iron Works when Jethro J. McCullough was a partner.

At the Centennial Exposition of 1876 the Philadelphia Architectural Iron Company entered a display of "galvanized iron and sheet zinc gate entrance." Among the other exhibitors of galvanized products were the McCullough Iron Company and three other Philadelphia firms. In the 1872 catalog the Philadelphia Architectural Iron Company also advertised multi-story galvanized sheet iron fronts, which were to become very popular at the turn of the century.

The catalog also suggests that the company manufactured the "Gilbert Patent Corrugated Iron Arched Ceilings" and that J. S. Thorn apparently owned the patents. There may have been other connections between Thorn and the Architectural Iron Works, for in a catalog published in the late 1880's, Thorn illustrated many of the identical cornices offered in the iron works catalog of 1872 as well as the corrugated iron ceilings. The Philadelphia Architectural Iron Company catalog is very typical of its contemporaries in the extensive listings of buildings where its products had been used. The fact that many of these were situated in the Midwest attests to how widely distributed such products had become by the 1870's.

The scale for the illustrations in the catalog is as follows:

SCALE OF DIMENSIONS

Plate 1   Any required size.
Plate 2   "   "   "
Plate 5 ⎫
Plate 6 ⎪
Plate 7 ⎪ $\frac{1}{2}$ inch to the foot.
Plate 8 ⎬
Plate 9 ⎪
Plate 10 ⎭
Plate 13 ⎫
Plate 14 ⎬ $\frac{1}{10}$th full size.
Plate 15 ⎭

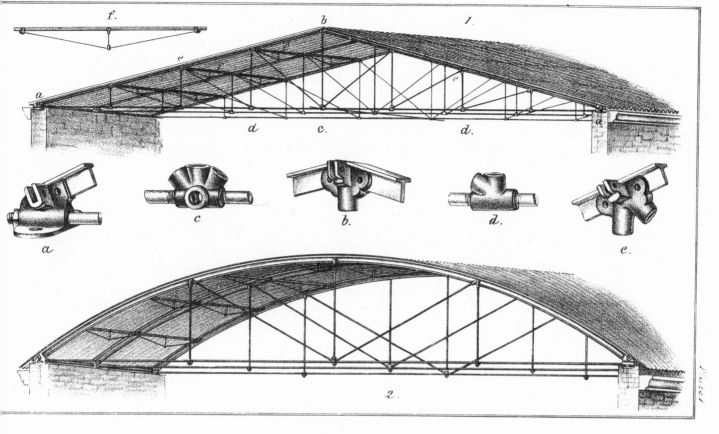

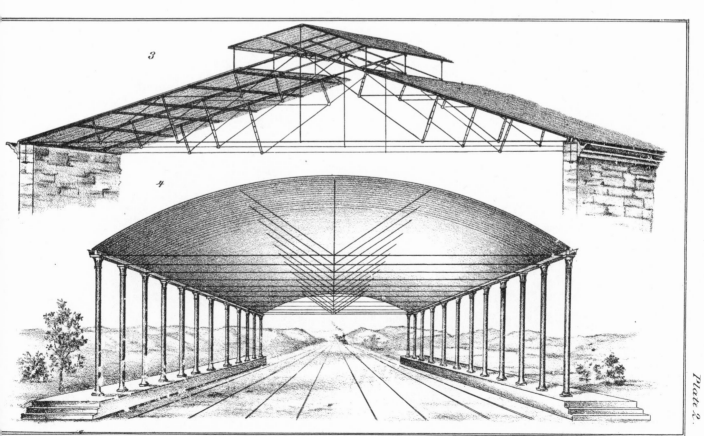

Plate 3.

Plate 4.

IRON TRUSS ROOFS.

We respectfully solicit the particular attention of Railroad Companies, Architects, and all others who require first-class, substantial buildings, to our Iron Truss Roofs.

After a full experience of many years as roof-engineers, and having abundant facilities for executing contracts for Iron Roofs, we are prepared to receive and execute orders for any specified plan or dimensions. We respectfully point to numerous iron roofs of our construction, as our best references of good workmanship. The dimensions and location of a few of these will be found on pages 10, 11, 12, 13 and 14.

We also manufacture skeletons or frames of iron for any covering which may be required. This includes Galvanized Corrugated Iron, or Painted Corrugated Iron, Slate, or Tin laid on boards. We are prepared to execute contracts for Railroad Buildings of every description, Engine Houses, Machine Shops, &c., &c. We append a list of some of the roofs which we have erected during our business career, all of which have given entire satisfaction.

We do not consider it necessary to give here a detailed description of the roof plates given, as the method of construction speaks for itself in the cuts. As no two roofs are alike, a definite estimate of cost can be given only after personal interview, or correspondence bearing on the contract in question.

The plates give our leading methods of roof construction.

No. 1 represents our independent truss.

No. 2. A trussed arched rafter, covered with curved corrugated sheets.

No. 3. A French truss; skylight attached.

No. 4. A simple arch, formed of curved corrugated sheets, without rafters or trusses of any kind, being merely tied and braced, as shown.

The latter style makes a very cheap covering, thoroughly substantial, for any span under 35 feet. We have constructed a number of small spans of this design, which have given entire satisfaction.

PLATE No. 3. Shows a locomotive round-house, framed with the independent truss rafter,—we have constructed a number of round-house roofs after this design,—the roof supported by the outside wall, and a circle of iron columns within. The Illinois Central Railroad, and Raleigh and Gaston Railroad engine-houses, are roofed after this plan—the former containing 18, the latter 20 engine-stalls.

PLATE No. 4, is from a photograph of the Union Depot Building at Atlanta, Ga.—span, 120 feet; length, 352 feet. All the work in this building above the walls, including towers, dormers, cornices, &c., is of our construction. The roof is after the trussed arch design, (plate No. 1,) and is covered with corrugated galvanized sheet iron; the towers are roofed with slate; the rafters in this roof are of curved deck beams, substantially trussed, tied and secured by anchors, purlins of **T** iron trussed—the principles of strength and durability being carried through the whole structure—and weight and resistance of material so balanced, that we feel safe in saying, there is not a more substantial roof covering in the country. We construct any of our frames to carry either flat or corrugated iron, slate or tin, at option of the buyer.

RAILROAD BUILDINGS.

PHILADELPHIA, WILMINGTON AND BALTIMORE RAILROAD COMPANY, at Baltimore, engine house, iron covering.

NORFOLK AND PETERSBURG RAILROAD COMPANY, at Norfolk, engine house, iron covering.

ILLINOIS CENTRAL RAILROAD COMPANY, at Chicago, engine house, iron covering.

ILLINOIS CENTRAL RAILROAD COMPANY, at Chicago, machine shop, 75 by 175, iron covering.

ILLINOIS CENTRAL RAILROAD COMPANY, at Chicago, blacksmith shop, 70 by 100, iron covering.

ILLINOIS CENTRAL RAILROAD COMPANY, at Centralia, Ill., car shop, iron covering.

ILLINOIS CENTRAL RAILROAD COMPANY, at Centralia, storehouse, iron covering.

LEHIGH COAL AND NAVIGATION COMPANY, at White Haven, Pa., engine house, iron covering.

CUMBERLAND VALLEY RAILROAD COMPANY, at Chambersburg, Pa., engine house, iron covering.

CHICAGO, BURLINGTON AND QUINCY RAILROAD COMPANY, at Chicago, Ill., engine house, iron covering.

CHICAGO, BURLINGTON AND QUINCY RAILROAD COMPANY, at Aurora, Ill., machine shop, iron covering.

CHICAGO, BURLINGTON AND QUINCY RAILROAD COMPANY, at Burlington, Iowa, engine house, 82 by 180, slate covering.

CAMDEN AND AMBOY RAILROAD COMPANY, at Amboy, N. J., oil house, iron covering.

RALEIGH AND GASTON RAILROAD COMPANY, at Raleigh, N. C., engine house, iron covering.

PHILADELPHIA, WILMINGTON AND BALTIMORE RAILROAD COMPANY, at Wilmington, Del., iron frame.

UNION DEPOT, Atlanta, Ga., fire proof building, 352 by 120 ft.

LEHIGH VALLEY RAILROAD, engine house, cast iron front, and iron roof frame.

FOUNDRYS, MACHINE SHOPS, ETC.

PHŒNIX IRON FOUNDRY, Phœnixville, Pa., iron covering.

CAR-WHEEL WORKS OF A. WHITNEY & SONS, Philadelphia, iron covering.

UNITED STATES ARSENAL, Frankford, Philadelphia, iron covering.

C. AULTMAN'S AGRICULTURAL WORKS, Canton, Ohio, 75 by 150, iron covering.

HOOPES & TOWNSEND, Philadelphia, blacksmith shop, iron covering.

JNO. FARNUM, Lancaster, Pa., engine house, iron covering.

METOACA MANUFACTURING COMPANY, Petersburg, Va., cotton mills, iron covering; three roofs.

BEMENT & DOUGHERTY, Philadelphia, pattern house, iron covering.

BEMENT & DOUGHERTY, Philadelphia, boiler house, iron covering.

T. W. HARVEY, Chicago, saw mill, iron covering.

WM. L. WILSON, Spring Mill, Pa., Terra Cotta Works, iron covering.

BALDWIN LOCOMOTIVE WORKS, Philadelphia, roof and ceilings.

JAS. KITCHENMAN, roof.

JAS. BROMLEY & BRO., two roofs.

JOLIET IRON AND STEEL COMPANY, Joliet, Ill., four roofs.

CHICAGO IRON COMPANY, iron roof frame and covering.

GAS WORKS.

BROOKLYN GAS-LIGHT COMPANY, Brooklyn, N. Y., retort house, slate covering.

BROOKLYN GAS-LIGHT COMPANY, Brooklyn, N. Y., purifying house, slate covering.

LEBANON GAS WORKS, Lebanon, Pa., slate covering.

READING GAS-LIGHT COMPANY, Reading, Pa., slate covering.

LANCASTER GAS WORKS, Lancaster, Pa., slate covering.

ELIZABETH GAS WORKS, Elizabeth, N. J., slate covering.

JERSEY CITY GAS-LIGHT COMPANY, Jersey City, N. J., slate covering.

COATESVILLE, PA., GAS WORKS, iron roof frame.

BANKS.

Enterprise Insurance Company, Philadelphia, cornices, window heads, &c.

Fulton Bank, Atlanta, Ga., iron covering.

Philadelphia Bank, Philadelphia, Pa., corrugated copper covering.

Banking House of Jay Cooke & Co., Washington, D. C., iron covering.

Lockhaven Bank, Lockhaven, Pa., iron covering and cornice.

Jersey Shore Bank, Jersey Shore, Pa., iron covering and cornice.

First National Bank, Chicago, iron ceiling and cornice.

COURT HOUSES, HOSPITALS, ETC.

Court House, Macon, Ga., cornice, &c.

Court House, Mobile, Ala., iron covering.

Macoupin County Court House, Carlinsville, Ill., iron covering.

United States Marine Hospital, New Orleans, iron covering and cornice.

United States Marine Hospital, Wilmington, N. C., iron covering and cornice.

Christ Church Hospital, Philadelphia, slate covering.

Barracks and Officers Quarters, Fort Delaware, iron covering and cornice.

WAREHOUSES, ETC.

Clement & Dunbar, Philadelphia, warehouse, iron covering.

Grigg's Building, Philadelphia, iron covering.

McCullough Iron Company, Philadelphia Galvanizing Works, iron covering.

Santa Catalina Warehouse, Havana, iron covering.

Two Storehouses, Havana, roofs and sides corrugated iron.

Lamp Black Houses, C. E. Johnson, Philadelphia, roofs and sides corrugated iron.

Smith & Harris, frame and covering, two roofs.

MARKETS.

| Eastern Market, Philadelphia, corrugated iron awning. |
| R. M. Arthur, " |
| Fairmount Market, " |
| Stephen Fagen, " |
| Western Market, " |
| Twenty-Fourth Ward Market, " |
| Farmers' Market, " |
| Twelfth Street Market, " |
| Central Market Company, " |
| Federal " " |
| Lincoln " " |

GALVANIZED IRON CORNICES.

The superior merits of Galvanized Iron Cornices are now well known to architects and builders. It is not, therefore, necessary to enter upon an elaborate description of their merits in order to inform them. But for the sake of presenting these merits more fully, before all those who are interested in buildings, we will briefly point out some things in which they excel all other descriptions of cornices.

From an experience of twenty years we can testify how gradually, but surely Galvanized Iron Cornices have come into favor. Their popularity is now so wide spread, that in order to answer the many personal and epistolary inquiries which are constantly made to us concerning cost and other particulars, we have been induced to offer to the public a catalogue of a portion of our patterns. The styles, however, are so numerous, subject, too, to other and newer, and, of course, to increasing improvements on these styles, that it is almost impossible to set them forth in one book.

We claim, first, as a primary merit for Galvanized Iron Cornices, their *cheapness*, compared with those of stone or cast iron. This alone should recommend them to builders generally, especially when strength and lightness are taken into the account, which can be easily shown.

Durability, as compared with wood, is another merit possessed by our cornices. Driving rains and atmospherical influences will hasten the decay of wooden cornices; but, as our Galvanized Iron Cornices will resist all climatic changes, they possess the merit of durability.

The *lightness* of the material is another recommendation in favor of Galvanized Iron Cornices. Their pressure on the walls of buildings is comparatively little, which makes them the more easily to be fitted to their places, and more safe and permanent in their positions.

We furnish Galvanized Cornices of any required design, either plain or of the most elaborate description.

FIRE-PROOF BUILDINGS.

Thorough fire-proof floors or ceilings, such as will prevent the spread of the flames from one floor to another, and which will confine the fire to the floor on which it originated, must be acknowledged to be a desideratum in the erection of all buildings, especially of large and public edifices. We now manufacture these ceilings, known as the Gilbert Patent Corrugated Iron Arched Ceilings, under letters patent granted within the last three years. We have carefully examined into the merits of this valuable ceiling or floor, and have been so convinced of the vast advantages of its peculiar construction that we can confidently recommend it to all architects and builders, and to all interested in building. We do this with more confidence, as it has been closely examined by the principal architects and engineers of this and other cities, and unanimously pronounced a most valuable invention.

The following advantages may be briefly stated in favor of the iron ceiling:

1. It takes fully one-half or more of the weight from the walls of the building.

2. The great strength of the corrugated iron arch enables us to place the beams wider apart than when brick is used, consequently its use will admit of beams of less weight being used, and fewer of them than is necessary with brick arches.

3. It saves the rods.

4. It saves plastering.

5. There is no lateral pressure against walls.

6. It is more ornamental than the plain brick arches.

These advantages, without adding a word more, are sufficient surely to introduce iron ceilings or floors to universal adaptation.

We may just add, that although this method of fire-proof ceiling has been brought to the notice of the public within the last three years, yet large orders have been received by us from all parts of the country, and in all buildings into which these ceilings have been introduced, they have given entire satisfaction.

REPORT FROM THE FRANKLIN INSTITUTE OF PENNSYLVANIA.

HALL OF THE FRANKLIN INSTITUTE,
PHILADELPHIA, *Feb.* 26, 1868.

The Committee on Science and the Arts, constituted by the Franklin Institute of the State of Pennsylvania, for the promotion of the Mechanic Arts, to whom was referred for examination a *Fire-Proof Ceiling invented by Mr.* JOSEPH GILBERT, report that the nature of the invention is in the use of CORRUGATED SHEET-IRON, supported upon, and spanning the space between iron beams, the corrugations being so arranged that a series of alternate convex and concave arches extend as ribs and depressions across the space between the beams, thus giving to the sheets vertical stiffness. The sheets are covered with cement, which increases this stiffness and prevents moisture from penetrating downwards to the iron. The sheets may extend straight from beam to beam, or may be arched as is customary with brick or concrete fire-proof floors.

When used as a flooring it is arched so that the top of its cement cover is nearly flush with that of the beams. Any description of floor may be laid on the beams. The intervening space between floor and arch may be filled with concrete, resting against haunches of brick placed next the sides of the beams. The corrugated sheets are secured to the beams (acting thus as ties or braces) by means of cast-iron ledges of suitable shape, resting upon the lower flanges of the beams, and fastened thereto.

It will be evident from this description that the distinguishing feature of the mode under discussion, as compared with other plans of fire-proof floors, is in the substitution of corrugated sheet-iron, covered with cement, for either brick or concrete arches, or for flat sheets of iron covered with cement.

The following advantages appear to be secured by it:

1st. A considerable reduction in the weight of the floor, which enables the beams to be lighter, and which, from both these causes, reduces the weight to be borne by the walls of the building.

2d. A saving of time in the execution of the work, and in scaffolding for completion of the building, as each story may be separately progressing without fear of accident, while the walls are laterally strengthened during the course of building.

3d. Some saving in story height may be affected, owing to the

reduced thickness of the arch, without increasing the number of beams employed.

So far as regards its fire-proof qualities, the Committee believe it to be fully equal to either of the modes commonly employed. Possessing the advantages already enumerated, its introduction in lieu of other systems will, in the opinion of the Committee, be governed by commercial considerations, into which they cannot of course enter. There does not appear to be any good reason why its expense should be greater than brick arches on iron beams.

By order of the Committee WM. HAMILTON, *Actuary.*

Messrs. J. VAUGHAN MERRICK,
THOS. S. STEWART, } *Committee of Examination.*
EDWIN F. DURANG,

The undersigned having examined the merits of the "GILBERT FIRE-PROOF CEILING," fully endorse the foregoing report of the Committee of Science and Arts of the Franklin Institute of Pennsylvania.

JOHN MCARTHUR, JR., *Architect,*
No. 205 South Sixth Street, Philadelphia.

JOHN STEWART, *Architect,*
No. 427 Walnut Street, Philadelphia.

SAMUEL SLOAN, *Architect,*
No. 152 South Fourth Street, Philadelphia.

JAMES H. WINDRIM, *Architect,*
No. 800 Walnut Street, Philadelphia.

JOHN FRASER, *Architect,*
No. 430 Walnut Street, Philadelphia.

GEORGE W. HEWITT, *Architect,*
No. 430 Walnut Street, Philadelphia.

FRANK FURNESS, *Architect,*
No. 430 Walnut Street, Philadelphia.

J. C. SYDNEY, *Architect,*
No. 204 South Fifth Street, Philadelphia.

ISAAC H. HOBBS & SON, *Architects,*
No. 436 Walnut Street, Philadelphia.

GEORGE SUMMERS, *Architect,*
No. 623 Walnut Street, Philadelphia.

S. D. BUTTON, *Architect,*
No. 430 Walnut Street, Philadelphia.

RICHARD B. OSBORNE, *Architect,*
Civil Engineer, Philadelphia.

The following Sketches or Diagrams will give a practical idea of the manner of using the Corrugated Arched Ceiling:

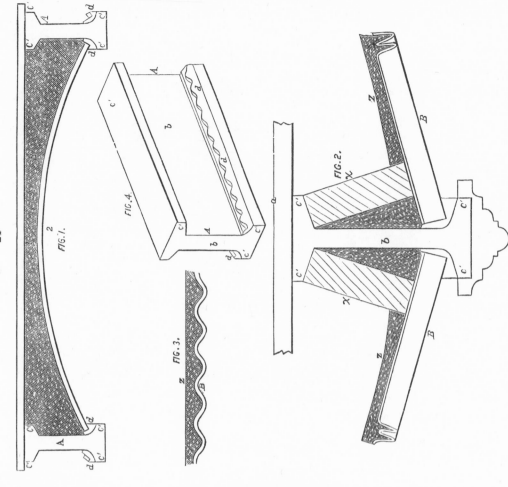

FIG.1.

FIG.4.

FIG.3.

FIG.2.

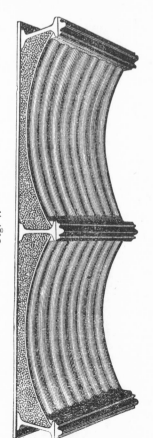

Fig. 7.

Fig. 7 illustrates two sections of the Corrugated Iron Arches, or part of a finished ceiling, with concrete to the surface of the beams, and the lower flange of the beams enclosed or covered with a galvanized iron casing, which makes a very ornamental finish.

Fig. 1 shows an elevation of this ceiling; two **H** beams, with corrugated arch between, resting on the lower flanges; inclined bricks at the haunches; the space between the bricks and beams filled with concrete, and a light layer of concrete upon the surface of the arched plates.

Fig. 2 is a detached sectional view of the same, on a large scale, showing one beam, with parts of the arches, brick haunches and concrete.

Fig. 3 is a section across sheet.

Fig. 5.—A corrugated iron ceiling, panelled and ornamented with centre pieces.

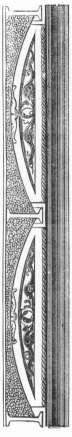

Fig. 6.

Fig. 6 is an end view of the same. Any style of ornamentation applied to suit the purchaser.

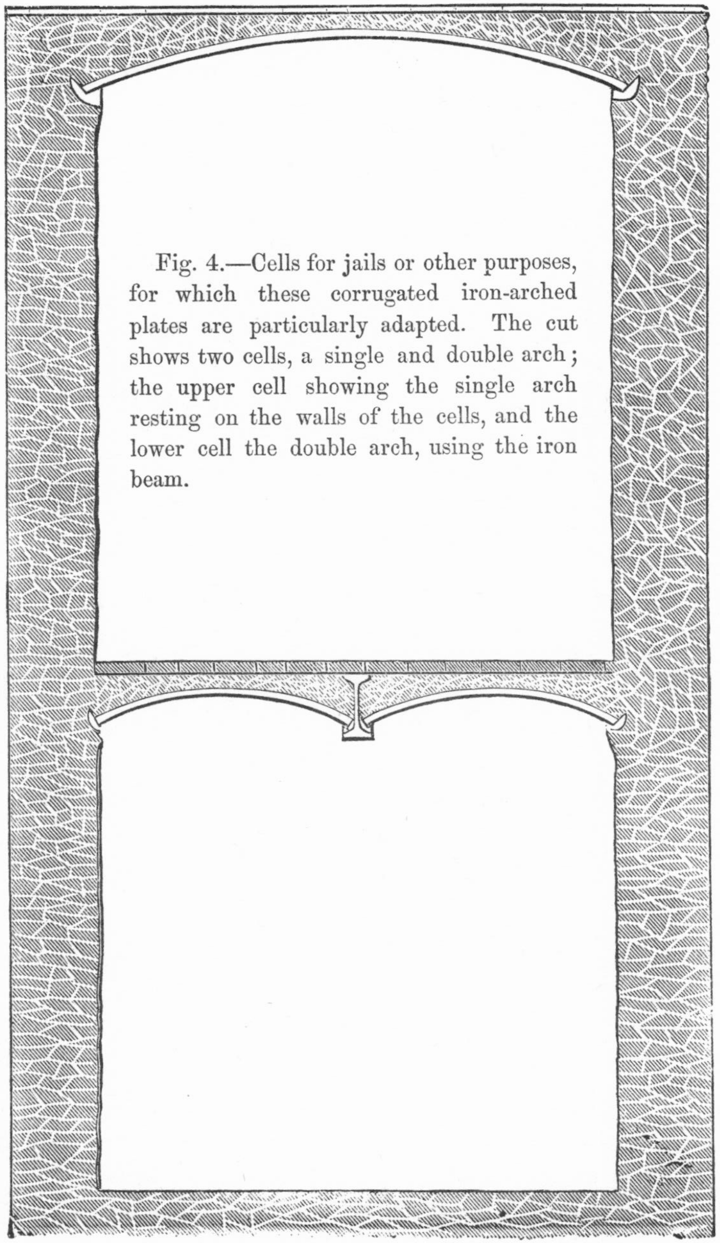

Fig. 4.—Cells for jails or other purposes, for which these corrugated iron-arched plates are particularly adapted. The cut shows two cells, a single and double arch; the upper cell showing the single arch resting on the walls of the cells, and the lower cell the double arch, using the iron beam.

We beg to call attention to the great strength of the Corrugated Iron Arch, as demonstrated by practical trials made, one at our own works, in the presence of J. C. Trautwine, Esq., civil engineer, and a number of our leading business men, and one at the Union Foundry Works, Chicago, Ill., as per certificate annexed of Messrs. N. S. Bouton & Co. The test at our works was continued through a period of several weeks, at various times, with the following result. A section of the Corrugated Iron Ceiling, made of a sheet of iron, No. 18 wire gauge, six feet, by twenty-eight inches, sustained over six tons, dead weight, on the arch itself, with a very slight deflection, not more than one-eighth of an inch.

UNION FOUNDRY WORKS,
CHICAGO, ILL., *May 20, 1868.*

DEAR SIR:—We had a test of the Iron Arches on Monday, 18th inst., in the presence of the Committee of the new "*Tribune* Buildings." Two sections of No. 16 iron arches, six feet long, and constructed as in the building, sustained upwards of nine tons weight, which was placed upon it.

The result was perfectly satisfactory, and an order given to put in the "ceiling."

Very truly yours,

N. S. BOUTON & CO.

Annexed please find list of a few of the buildings into which the Iron Ceilings have been introduced:

MESSRS. TATHAM & BROTHERS, Lead Pipe Works, Philadelphia.
MESSRS. HOWELL & BROTHERS, Wall Paper Warehouse, "
INSANE ASYLUM, Harrisburg, Pa.
CHICAGO TRIBUNE CO., PRINTING HOUSE, Chicago, Ill.
FIRST NATIONAL BANK, Chicago, Ill.
NORTHWESTERN MUTUAL LIFE INSURANCE CO., Milwaukee, Wis.
MACOUPIN COUNTY COURT HOUSE, Carlinsville, Ill.
QUEEN ANN'S COUNTY JAIL, Maryland.
INSANE ASYLUM, Iowa.

The following highly respectable testimonials, addressed to Mr. J. S. Thorn, the present owner of the Patent Corrugated Iron Ceiling, the work in every instance having been executed by us as manufacturing agents, will be sufficient to show the entire satisfaction the ceilings have given wherever used.

OFFICE OF THE TRIBUNE,
CHICAGO, *June 15, 1869.*
J. S. THORN, ESQ.,
Philadelphia, Pa.
SIR:—The new building of the "Tribune Co." is constructed with Gilbert Corrugated Ceiling, and our confidence in the ceiling is such that we consider that it renders the building practically fire-proof. In appearance it is ornamental. We recommend it to those contemplating the construction of fire-proof buildings.
TRIBUNE CO.,
By A. COWLES, Sec'y.

FIRST NATIONAL BANK,
CHICAGO, *June 15, 1869.*
J. S. THORN, ESQ.,
No. 429 Walnut Street, Philadelphia.
DEAR SIR:—Having used in the construction of our new banking house your Gilbert Patent Corrugated Iron Ceiling throughout, rendering the building strictly fire-proof, we are gratified to inform you that we consider this method of fire-proof floors superior to anything heretofore produced, and cheerfully render this our endorsement of its merits.
Very truly, &c.,
SAML. M. NICKERSON, Pres't.

PHILADELPHIA, *January 3, 1870.*
MR. J. S. THORN,
It gives us pleasure to state that the Patent Iron Arched Ceiling, introduced by you into our new fire-proof warehouse, Nos. 12 and 14 South Sixth Street, answers every purpose, and we have no hesitation in recommending it to those contemplating erecting fire-proof structures.
Yours, &c.
HOWELL & BROTHERS,
Manufacturers of Wall Papers.

MILWAUKEE, *Feb. 7, 1870.*
J. S. THORN, ESQ.,
DEAR SIR:—We have used the Gilbert Corrugated Ceiling in the new building erected for the Northwestern Mutual Life Insurance Co. We consider it practically as fire-proof as the brick arch, and recommend its use in the construction of fire-proof buildings.
NORTHWESTERN MUTUAL LIFE INS. CO.
By J. C. SPENCER.

Galvanized Sheet Iron Architecture.

To make our catalogue more complete, we append the following plates, Nos. 16, 17 and 18, to give an idea of the appearance of sheet iron architecture.

Plate No. 16, gives a view of the dome of the Macoupin County Court House, Illinois, erected by us about three years since, is of iron throughout. Extreme diameter, 45 feet; height from main roof to base of lantern, 65 feet; height from main roof to top of spire, 125 feet. We erected a large amount of ornamental work, both in the interior pannelling and finish of the rooms, and the interior and exterior of the dome. An examination of the finish of the dome, shows how we apply our ornamental stamped work, being elaborately ornamented with brackets, Corinthian columns, scrolls, mouldings, leaf work, &c., nearly all of which are of galvanized sheet iron, combining the smallest amount of weight with durability.

FRENCH ROOFS, DORMERS, &c.

We are prepared to contract for and construct, French or Mansard roofs of all styles, plain or elaborate, of galvanized sheet throughout, or part sheet and part slate. Nos. 17 and 18 show French roofs with dormers, towers, &c., complete of our construction. It is not necessary that any woodwork should enter into the construction of this class of architecture, as we can, when desired, back it with a light iron frame, and stiffen where necessary, with light braces, so that it is perfectly practicable to do away with the great objection to the Mansard roof, its liability to fire, as we make them all iron above the walls.

IRON FRONTS.

We are prepared to contract for and erect, in any part of the country, fronts for stores and public buildings, &c., of SHEET OR CAST iron, or in part of each. Our customers find it expedient at times to have a first story of cast iron for strength, the balance of galvanized sheet iron backed with rough brick work, combining lightness and security from fire, with any required design, and at a less cost, considering the durability of the work, than can be produced in any other way.

We have now presented in this volume, as complete an outline of our business as we can. We claim to do a larger class of work than any other house in the country. We are prepared to construct or supply *any material* appertaining to iron architecture, to supply sets of beams and rafters for warehouses, or special iron work of any description. We claim that it is of advantage to any builder to be able to manufacture the several items of roofs, cornices, fronts, beams, &c., and to adapt them to each other in the same factory, rather than to divide the job among several manufacturers, trusting to the correspondence of parts when brought together.

We guarantee to make of sheet iron, any style of construction that can be carved in stone or cast, losing none of the advantages of those materials, and gaining some that they have not, such as cheapness, lightness, with a proportionally less cost of transportation, and an equally good, if not better appearance when finished.

By the introduction into our works of greatly improved machinery, we are enabled to produce the most elaborate designs at comparatively small cost. Our house is one of the oldest in the country, having been established now fully 20 years, which gives us the benefit of a very extensive experience in our business, and a set of operatives, fully acquainted with every detail of their trade, to be acquired only by years of practice, so that we know our work to be unsurpassed by that of any other firm.

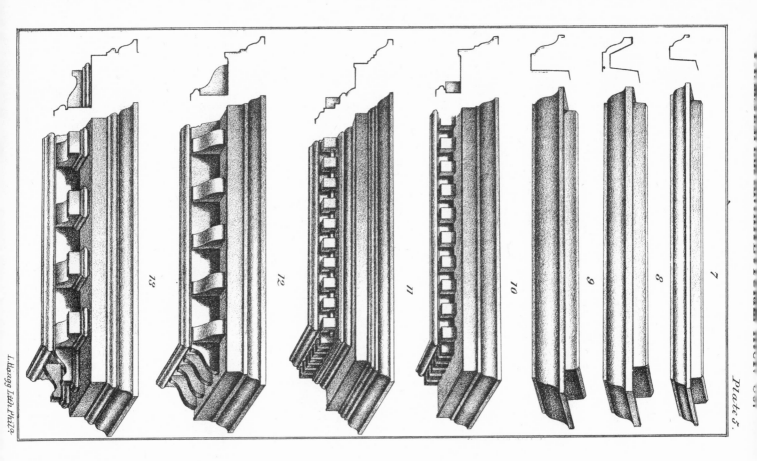

Plate 5.

13   12   11   10   9   8   7

14

15

Plate 6.

L.Haugg Lith.Phil.

16

17

19

18

20

Plate 9.

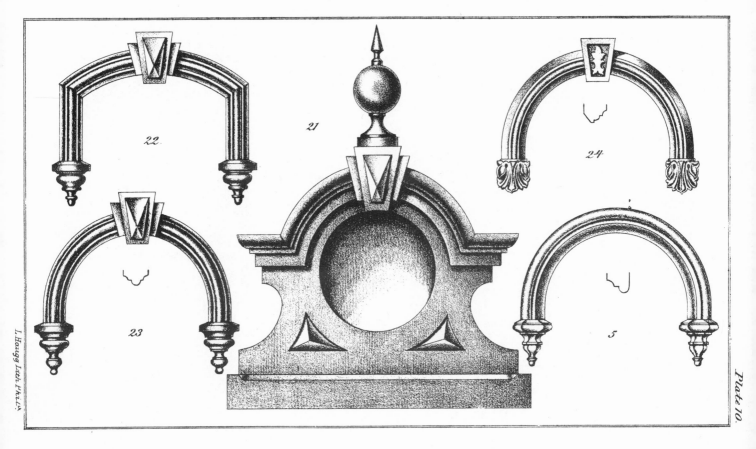

22.

21

24.

23

5

Plate 10.

Plate 12.

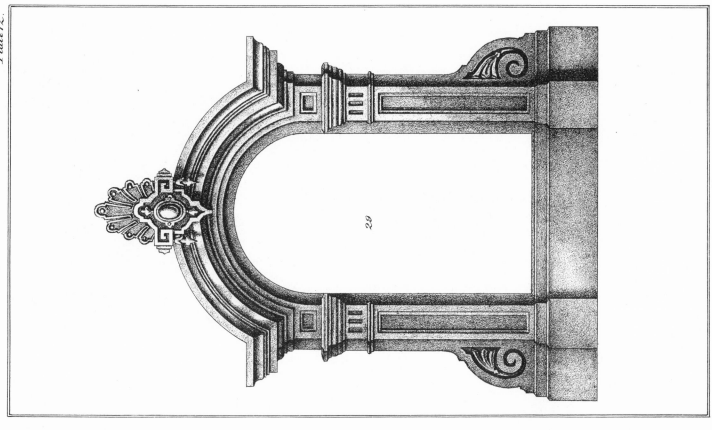

Plate 11.

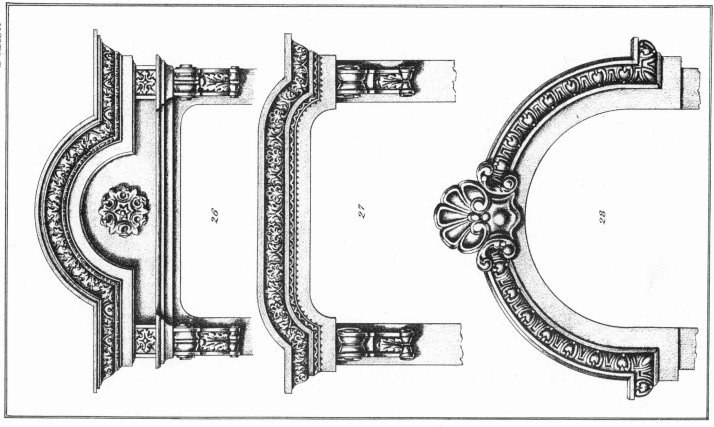

Plate 16.

PHILADELPHIA ARCHITECTURAL IRON CO.

Plate 13.

PHILADELPHIA ARCHITECTURAL IRON CO.

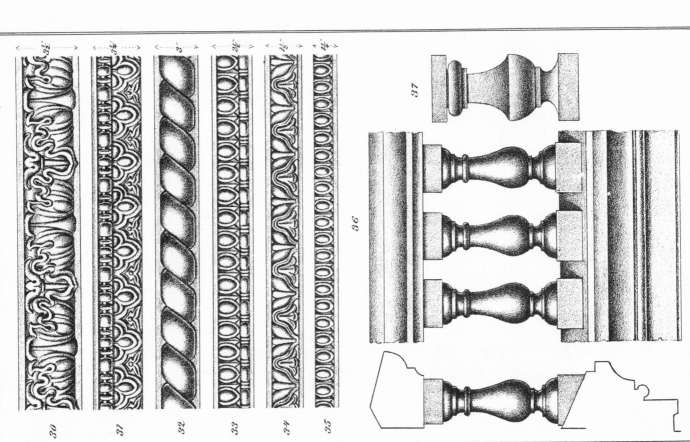

30

31

32

33

34

35

36

37

Plate 14.

38

39

40

41

42

43

44

45

46

47

48

49

50

51

52

53

45

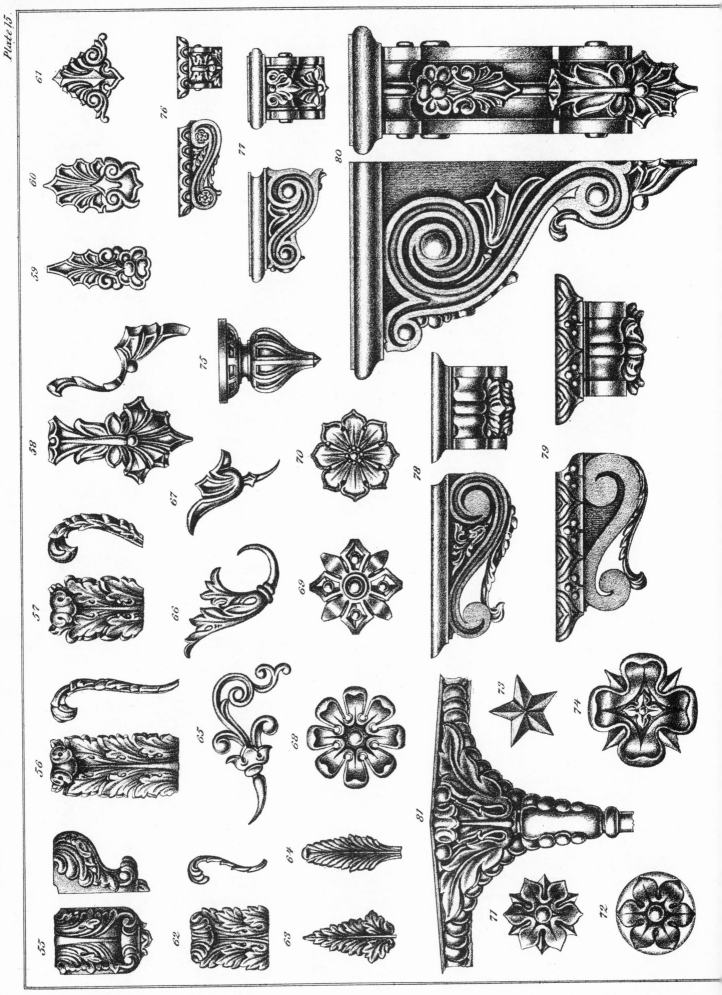

Plate 15.

PHILADELPHIA ARCHITECTURAL IRON CO.

Plate 17.

PHILADELPHIA ARCHITECTURAL IRON CO.

Plate 18

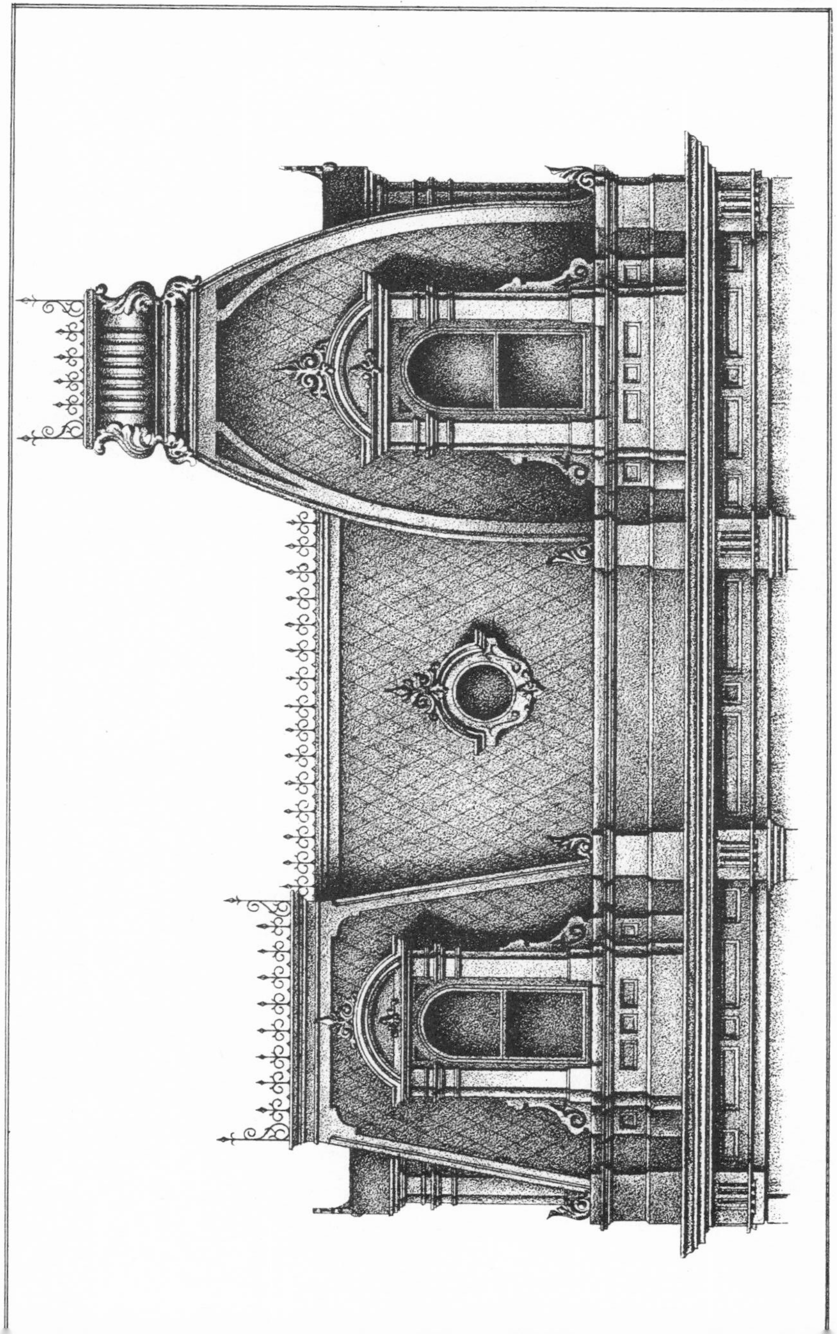

FIRE-PROOF CONSTRUCTION.

LOCOMOTIVE ENGINE HOUSE.

PHILADELPHIA ARCHITECTURAL IRON COMPANY,

11th and Washington Avenue, Philadelphia.

L.HAUGG. PHILA.

KEYSTONE SLATE MANTEL

The firm of Wilson & Miller, proprietors of the Keystone Slate Mantel and Slate Works had its beginnings in 1853, when S. A. Harrison offered for sale in Philadelphia marbleized slate mantels that had been made in New England. Three years later he sold the business to W. A. Arnold and John W. Wilson, which then became Arnold & Wilson, and began manufacturing marbleized slate mantels on Chestnut Street. In 1863 the partnership was dissolved.

After serving two years in the Civil War, Wilson opened another factory and in 1868 became associated with Joseph S. Miller, who had just completed his apprenticeship as a marble worker. The firm was known as Wilson & Miller through 1878. Its prosperity was explained thus in 1875:

> Like other novelties, slate-wares had to pass through a critical ordeal, and to be tested both by time and use. It was a work of no small difficulty to overcome the prejudices of those who deemed the cold white Italian marble mantel the beau-ideal of perfection and the only proper and necessary appendage of the aristocratic mansion. But by the gradual growth of a better taste for beauty and harmony of colors, the slate mantel has established its reputation in the community and now takes care of itself.

This account also suggests that Wilson & Miller obtained slab slate used for the mantels from Vermont quarries, but other sources indicate that they may also have used slate from Lehigh County, Pennsylvania.

The manufacturing process in the Wilson & Miller factory was described in 1875:

> The slate is received from the quarry in its rough state. First it is subjected to the cutting process, which is principally done by chisel and mallet. The necessary ornamentation and carving follows, and, these being effected, it is ready for the "marbleizer." The process is a secret, and known only to but few persons in the country. So rare is this accomplishment that the workman who is an adept in his peculiar business commands a highly remunerative salary; and the manufacturer himself is totally unacquainted with the details of the process. By the action of different powerful chemicals to the surface of the slab, the color is changed. This process occupies about six days; when completed, the polisher steps in, and by the necessary friction imparts a glossy surface, presenting to the eye of the observor the most perfect imitation of marbles of every description.

Wilson & Miller exhibited marbleized slate products, including mantels, as well as plain slate work at the Centennial Exposition.

Apparently about 1879 the firm was dissolved. John W. Wilson was listed in the city directories as dealing in stoves and ranges, not surprisingly since Wilson & Miller had carried a line of heaters, as had the firm's founder, S. A. Harrison. Miller continued the slate business under his name until 1884 when the firm became known as Joseph S. Miller & Brother. Between 1893 and 1896 Miller again operated under his own name. In 1898 he entered the tile business, which later became known as Joseph S. Miller & Co. and finally passed into the hands of a receiver about 1916.

CARD

In publishing this, the revised edition of our *Illustrated Catalogue of Slate Mantels* and *other Slate Work*, we deem it unnecessary to go into an elaborate treatise on *Slate;* its uses and advantages over other stone for house decoration and building purposes. *Our efforts for the past eighteen years,* we flatter ourselves, have not been in vain, in calling the attention of *Architects, Builders* and the public to its various and appropriate uses. Marbleized Slate has established its claim as an object of beauty and utility, and is now fully acknowledged to be superior to *marble* or any *other stone,* for inside purposes: and in its plain state, for all use where exposure and durability are necessary.

We have added many new and beautiful designs, of Decorated Gold, Ebony, Rose and other beautiful colors, and in the Marbleizing represent each and every shade of *Marble, Stone* or *Wood,* as desired. Being the *first* to introduce the *Manufacture of Marbleized Slate* in *Pennsylvania,* we flatter ourselves, that in our determination to execute none but the very best work, we have secured the confidence of all who have favored us with their patronage. It is our determination to persevere in this course, feeling that the public appreciate good work and fair dealing.

WILSON & MILLER.

Philadelphia, 1872.

———o———

Particular attention given to laying *Slate Pavements* and *Tiling,* in all its branches.

Section for Vestibules and Wainscoating.

The Chocolate shade, represents Spanish.
The Black and Yellow shade, represents Egyptian.
The Green shade, represents Verde Antique.

And are the three leading colors in Marbleized work.

NEW GRECIAN ORDER.

Richly carved and decorated in gold.   Made to any size.

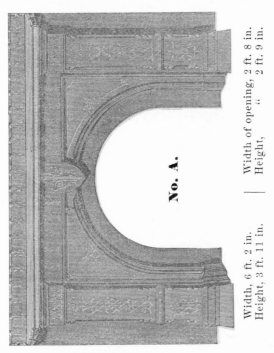

Width of opening, 2 ft. 8 in.
"   2 ft. 9 in.
Height,

No. A.

Width, 6 ft. 2 in.
Height, 3 ft. 11 in.

This is a most beautiful Mantel for drawing-room or parlor. Designed expressly for us, by Messrs. FURNESS & HEWITT, Architects of
this city. Executed by us in black and gilt, or other desired shade,
as Rosewood, Walnut, &c. Made to any size.

NEW GRECIAN ORDER,

Beautifully carved and decorated in gold.   Made to any size.

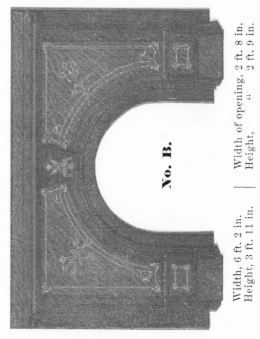

Width of opening, 2 ft. 8 in.
"   2 ft. 9 in.
Height,

No. B.

Width, 6 ft. 2 in.
Height, 3 ft. 11 in.

An elegant Parlor Mantel, also designed by Messrs. FURNESS &
HEWITT of this city, (as most of this class of our gold decorated work
is,) and finished in Ebony, Rosewood, Black Walnut, &c. Made to
any size.

GOLD DECORATED.

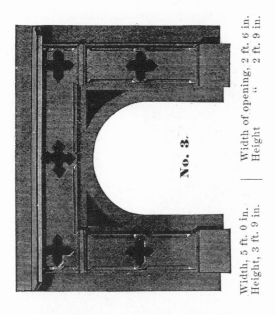

No. 3.

Width of opening, 2 ft. 6 in.
" Height 2 ft. 9 in.

Width, 5 ft. 0 in.
Height, 3 ft. 9 in.

A very pretty pattern in black ground, gold carvings and verde antique, as represented in cut.

FRENCH ARCH.

NEW STYLE, IN ANY SIZE.

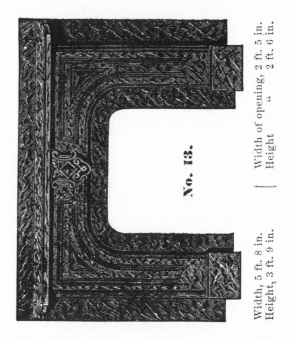

No. 13.

Width of opening, 2 ft. 5 in.
" Height 2 ft. 6 in.

Width, 5 ft. 8 in.
Height, 3 ft. 9 in.

In Spanish, with Verde Antique panel as here represented. A very handsome parlor Mantel.

Slate Mantels are more beautiful and much stronger than marble.

No. 12.

Width of opening, 2 ft. 6 in.
Height, " 2 ft. 8 in.

Width, 6 ft. 4 in.
Height, 4 ft.

A massive and beautiful Mantel for a large parlor or Banking House.

NEW GRECIAN.
GOLD DECORATED MANTEL.

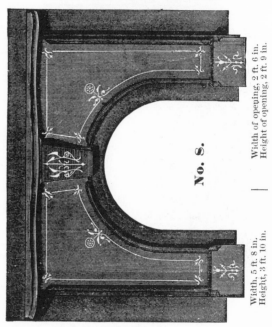

No. 8.

Width of opening, 2 ft. 6 in.
Height of opening, 2 ft. 9 in.

Width, 5 ft. 8 in.
Height, 3 ft. 10 in.

All the Gold Decorated Mantels shown in this Catalogue in white lines on a black ground, will, in the finished Mantels, be represented in gilt lines on a rosewood, ebony, walnut or other desirable shades.

Coal Gas or Smoke will not stain them.

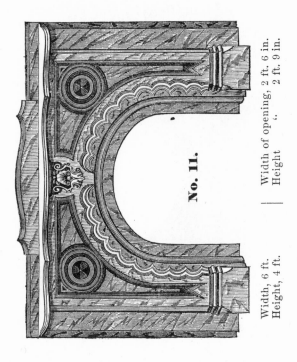

No. 11.

Width of opening, 2 ft. 6 in.
Height " 2 ft. 9 in.

Width, 6 ft.
Height, 4 ft.

An elaborately cut Mantel, desirable for Parlor, Drawing-room, &c.

NEW GRECIAN.

GOLD DECORATED MANTEL.

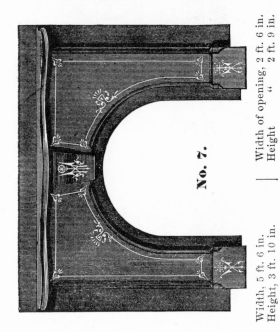

No. 7.

Width of opening, 2 ft. 6 in.
Height " 2 ft. 9 in.

Width, 5 ft. 6 in.
Height, 3 ft. 10 in.

Very rich, in black, rosewood or walnut.

NEW GRECIAN.

GOLD DECORATED.

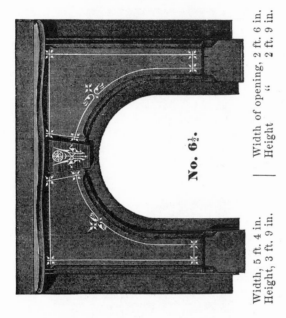

No. 6½.

Width of opening, 2 ft. 6 in.
" Height 2 ft. 9 in.

Width, 5 ft. 4 in.
Height, 3 ft. 9 in.

The Cars on Ridge Avenue; the Union Line on Spring Garden Street, pass the Store and Factory both ways. The cars on Twelfth Street, pass near the door; Cars on Green, Eleventh and Thirteenth Streets, pass within one square.

Every description of Marbleized or Plain Slate Work made to order.

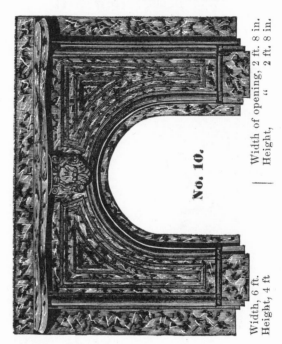

No. 10.

Width of opening, 2 ft. 8 in.
" Height, 2 ft. 8 in.

Width, 6 ft.
Height, 4 ft

A bold and beautiful design for parlor or other large room. Having bold recess circles, and heavy rounded corner returns. Very desirable.

NEW GRECIAN.
GOLD DECORATED MANTEL.
In Rosewood or Black.   Very neat.

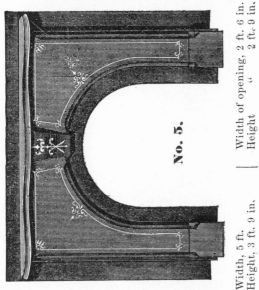

No. 5.

Width of opening, 2 ft. 6 in.
" Height " 2 ft. 9 in.

Width, 5 ft.
Height, 3 ft. 9 in.

The Cars on Ridge Avenue; the Union Line on Spring Garden St. pass the Store and Factory, both ways   The Cars on Twelfth Street, pass near the door; Cars on Green, Eleventh and Thirteenth Streets, pass within one square.

Mantels in Imitation of Spanish, Verde Antique, Egyptian, or any other Marble, Same Price.

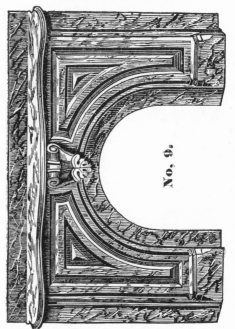

No. 9.

Width of opening, 2 ft. 7 in.
" Height " 2 ft. 8 in.

Width, 5 ft. 10 in.
Height, 3 ft. 10 in.

The Cars on Ridge Avenue; the Union Line on Spring Garden Street, pass the Store and Factory both ways. The Cars on Twelfth Street, pass near the door; Cars on Green, Eleventh and Thirteenth Streets, pass within one square.

NEW GRECIAN.

GOLD DECORATED.

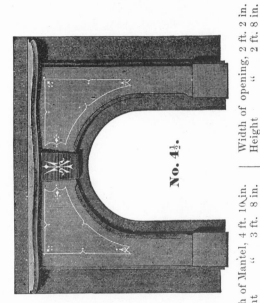

No. 4½.

Width of opening, 2 ft. 2 in.
Height " 2 ft. 8 in.

Width of Mantel, 4 ft. 10 in.
Height " 3 ft. 8 in.

The Cars on Ridge Avenue; the Union Line on Spring Garden Street, pass the Store and Factory both ways. The Cars on Twelfth Street, pass near the door; Cars on Green Eleventh and Thirteenth Streets, pass within one square.

SLATESTONE HEARTHS.

The Slate Hearth is the strongest and best that can be used.

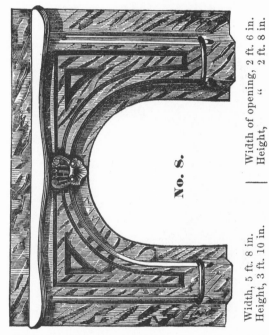

No. 8.

Width of opening, 2 ft. 6 in.
Height, " 2 ft. 8 in.

Width, 5 ft. 8 in.
Height, 3 ft. 10 in.

The Cars on Ridge Avenue; the Union Line on Spring Garden Street, pass the Store and Factory both ways. The Cars on Twelfth Street, pass near the door; Cars on Green, Eleventh and Thirteenth Streets, pass within one square.

This Mantel is made in imitation of Rosewood and Gold, with Black Panneling. New design, and is very rich.

No. 4.

Width of opening, 2 ft. 6 in.
" Height 2 ft. 10 in.

Width, 5 ft. 6 in.
Height, 3 ft. 10 in.

A very desirable Mantel for dining or other good size room. In Rosewood ground, inlaid in black, as represented in dark shades, and gilt lines.

CHURCH PULPITS OF MARBLEIZED SLATE,
Very Beautiful in Designs and Finish.

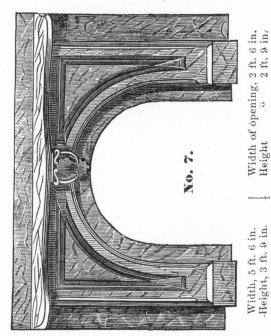

No. 7.

Width of opening, 2 ft. 6 in.
" Height 2 ft. 9 in.

Width, 5 ft. 6 in.
Height, 3 ft. 9 in.

The Cars on Ridge Avenue; the Union Line on Spring Garden Street, pass the Store and Factory both ways. The Cars on Twelfth Street, pass near the door; Cars on Green, Eleventh and Thirteenth Streets, pass within one square.

COUNTERS AND COUNTER TOPS,
Suitable for Banks, Stores Offices, &c.

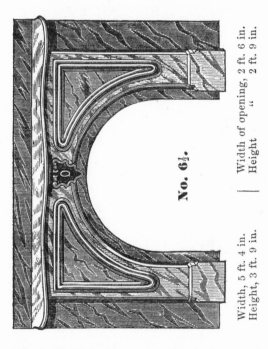

No. 6½.

Width of opening, 2 ft. 6 in.
" Height " 2 ft. 9 in.

Width, 5 ft. 4 in.
Height, 3 ft. 9 in.

This in Spanish Egyptian or Verde Antique, is a very pretty Mantel for a moderate size room.

Fireboards, all sizes and in imitation of any Marble.

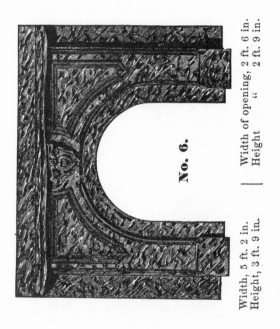

No. 6.

Width of opening, 2 ft. 6 in.
" Height " 2 ft. 9 in.

Width, 5 ft. 2 in.
Height, 3 ft. 9 in.

This is also a desirable Mantel, in any color, for a small parlor or sitting-room.

PLAIN SLATE SLABS, SHELVES FOR KITCHEN RANGES, TOPS OF WASHSTANDS, &c.

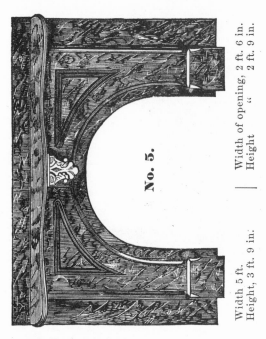

No. 5.

Width of opening, 2 ft. 6 in.
" Height 2 ft. 9 in.

Width 5 ft.
Height, 3 ft. 9 in.

To admit of a Baltimore Fire Place Stove or usual size grate, requires the opening to be as large as the opening of this Mantel.

Tiling and Flags for Floors and Pavements.

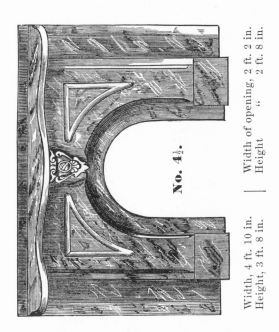

No. 4½.

Width of opening, 2 ft. 2 in.
" Height 2 ft. 8 in.

Width, 4 ft. 10 in.
Height, 3 ft. 8 in.

A neat Mantel for a bed-room. Opening not large enough for the ordinary size Baltimore or fire-place Stove.

Where a Mantel is required for a small Chimney breast in connection with a Baltimore Stove, this design can only be used, as it admits of the frame of the stove lapping on the front of the mantel, and at the same time makes a proper finish.

No. 0.

Width of opening, 2 ft. 6 in.
Height, " 2 ft. 8 in.

Width, 4 ft. 6 in.
Height, 3 ft. 8 in.

The Cars on Ridge Avenue; the Union Line on Spring Garden Street, pass the Store and Factory both ways. The Cars on Twelfth Street, pass near the door; Cars on Green, Eleventh and Thirteenth Streets, pass within one square.

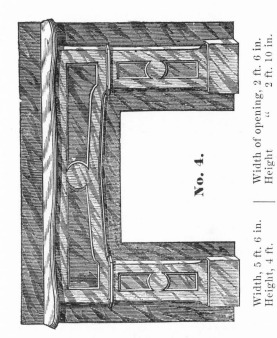

No. 4.

Width of opening, 2 ft. 6 in.
Height " 2 ft. 10 in.

Width, 5 ft. 6 in.
Height, 4 ft.

Desirable style for a dining or sitting room.

Handsome Pedestals and Columns for
Statuary, Bronzes, &c.

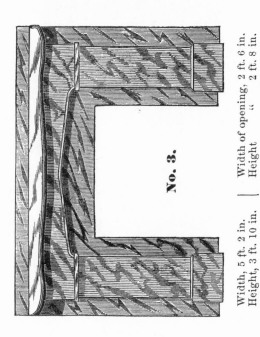

No. 3.

Width of opening, 2 ft. 6 in.
Height   "   2 ft. 8 in.

Width, 5 ft. 2 in.
Height, 3 ft. 10 in.

A plain and neat pattern for chambers.

NEW STYLES! SUPERIOR WORKMANSHIP!
LOW PRICES!

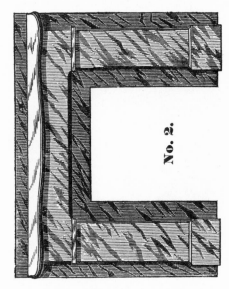

No. 2.

Width of opening, 2 ft. 6 in.
Height   "   2 ft. 8 in.

Width, 4 ft. 10 in.
Height, 3 ft. 9 in.

The Cars on Ridge Avenue; the Union Line on Spring Garden Street, pass the Store and Factory both ways. The Cars on Twelfth Street, pass near the door; Cars on Green, Eleventh and Thirteenth Streets, pass within one square.

Patent Hot-Air Registers and Ventilators.
All sizes.

Marbleized Register Facings,
Any size or color required.

Wash Tubs, Bath Tubs, Kitchen Sinks, &c.

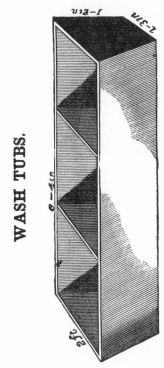

WASH TUBS.

The advantages of Slate over all other stone or wood for this purpose, is its non-absorbent qualities, consequently, can always be kept clean and sweet.

KITCHEN AND OTHER SINKS, any size desired.

NOTHING EQUAL TO SLATE FOR THIS PURPOSE.

THE LOW DOWN GRATE.

Has a Cast Iron Niche, with Firebrick Lining,
and set so that the fire will be on a level
with the hearth, with ash-pit and
draft from cellar. Well adapted
for all kinds of fuel.

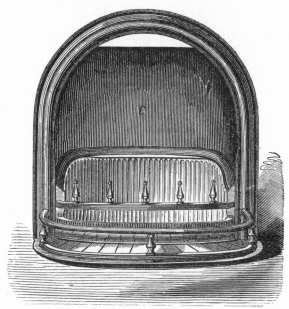

5 sizes, circular or square fronts.

ELEVATED FIRE GRATE.

For upper rooms or where ash-pits cannot be used.

5 sizes, square or circular opening.

Cast Niche and Fire-brick linings. Same as in low down grate, and with ash pan underneath. 5 sizes. Square or circular opening.

BASKET GRATE.

This is the old fashioned grate, well known to the public, will burn all kinds of fuel. Any size.

Niche or Cast Iron Fireplace for burning wood.

"In one room, at least, in every house there should be the exhilarating air and influence of an open fire.

I have seen respectability and amiability grouped over the air-tight stove; I have seen virtue and intelligence hovering over the register; but I have never seen true happiness in the family circle where the faces were not illuminated by the blaze of an open fire-place."

DR. OLIVER WENDELL HOLMES.

BALTIMORE STOVE.

Base Burner.

THE BEST FIREPLACE HEATER, warming the room in which it stands, and two or three rooms up stairs.

Our house being the first to introduce into this City the manufacture of these beautiful *Marbleized* Slate Mantles, and Slate Work generally. We bring to our business, a personal and practical experience of eighteen years that enables us to guarantee our work to be executed in the very best manner.

Our Marbleized Slate is a beautiful and durable representation of the most rare and choice marbles: Such as Spanish, Egyptian, Verde Antique Brocatel, Lisbon Sienna, Tennessee, Plymouth Black Porphyry, &c., the resemblance being so perfect as to challenge detection.

They have been awarded the GOLD MEDAL at the exhibitions of the AMERICAN INSTITUTE, *New York*; MASSACHUSETTS MECHANIC CHARITABLE ASSOCIATION, *Boston*; MARYLAND INSTITUTE, *Baltimore*; the PENN-SYLVANIA STATE FAIRS, and the FRANKLIN INSTITUTE of this City.

Mantles made to suit any size chimney breast, or design required.

Price List of Marbleized Slate Mantels.

No. 0, 4 feet 6 in. $	No. 6½, 5 feet 4 in. $
" 1, 4 " 6 "	" 7, 5 " 6 "
" 2, 4 " 10 "	" 8, 5 " 8 "
" 3, 5 " 0 "	" 9, 5 " 10 "
" 4, 5 " 6 "	" 10, 6 " 0 "
" 4½, 4 " 10 "	" 11, 6 " 0 "
" 5, 5 " 0 "	" 12, 6 " 4 "
" 6, 5 " 2 "	" 13, 5 " 8 "

Price List of the New Grecian Designs of Gold Decorated Mantels, &c.

No. 3, 5 feet $	No. 7, 5 feet 6 in. $
" 4, 5 " 6 in.	" 8, 5 " 8 "
" 4½, 4 " 10 "	" A, 6 " 2 "
" 5, 5 " 0 "	" B, 6 " 2 "
" 6½, 5 " 4 "	

These are new and beautiful designs, represented in Ebony and Gold, Rosewood and Gold, or inlaid in various colored Marble, with Gold decorations.

Any of the above Mantles, made larger or smaller as required.

Bracket Shelves, Serpentine Edges, per. single foot . . . . . $

Fireboards, regular size for our Mantles, each . . . . .

Fireboards, extra, according to size

Furniture Tops, as to design, per square foot . . . . .

Hearth for Stoves, Grates, Kitchen Ranges, &c., per foot . . .

Boxing extra, as to size.

Price List of Register Stones, &c.

8 inch,	$1 75	9x14 inches,	$2 75
9 "	2 00	10x10 "	2 75
10 "	2 30	10x14 "	3 00
12 "	2 75	10½x16½ "	3 50
14 "	3 50	12x12 "	3 00
16 "	4 50	12x15 "	3 50
18 "	5 75	12x19 "	5 00
20 "	7 50	14x22 "	6 00
24 "	12 00	15x25 "	7 00
6x8 "	1 75	16x24 "	7 00
8x10 "	2 00	20x26 "	9 00
8x12 "	2 25	27x38 "	15 00
8x18 "	3 00	30x30 "	15 00
9x12 "	2 50		

Side wall facings for circular top or other Registers, Marbleized to represent any Marbles or Wood as desired.

16x17 inches,	$15 00	12x17 inches,	$12 00
13x15 "	12 00	10x14 "	10 00
11x13 "	10 00	9x12 "	8 00

REGISTER STONES made of SLATE, are much *neater* and *better* than *Soap Stone*, and are *very much* STRONGER.

Hearths for Grates, Stoves, Kitchen Ranges, and other purposes.

Stationary Washtubs, in three compartments.

Kitchen Sinks, and Slate for any other purpose.

N B. Work put up in the city, or any part of the country by competent workmen, and warranted to give satisfaction.

WILSON & MILLER,

Directions for Setting up Mantels.

1st. Ascertain the width and height of Mantel. Cut off the plaster from the wall or partition, against which the mantel plates, shelf and head strips go. Set up the wall-plates the exact distance of the length of shelf, fastening them in their place with calcined plaster.

2d. Put up the fronts so that they touch in the center, this will show their position; now cut holes in the breast of chimney to correspond with holes in edge of mantel; make a hook of stout wire, drop one end into the hole in mantel, the other end anchored secure into wall or partition, first having plumbed, leveled and squared the fronts, now screw on the center or key.

3d. Place the fireboard and circles inside the opening, bring them up to their place, and fasten them with sticks, until properly secured with calcined plaster and masonry. If a *Stove* or *Grate* is to be set in, all the space between the breast of chimney and mantel *must* be built up *solid*. When a fire-board is used, solid work is not necessary, but enough to keep all firm in their places.

4th. Put on the shelf and head strip with a little calcined plaster on back of head strip and edge of shelf. Your mantel is now up.

Do not use plaster between the joints of mantel. If the joints require a little filling up, do it with common putty, the shade of the mantel.

When you can, always set the mantel down below the surface of the floor or hearth, more or less, it holds it in its place, and prevents its working out by the springing of the floor.

In Cleaning Mantels, wash with sponge and cold water, and dry with a damp chamois skin.

GEORGE O. STEVENS & CO., 1879

George O. Stevens & Co. was established in Baltimore in 1855 during a decade when American sash and blind factories doubled in number. This catalog of 1879 dates from an especially prosperous era of sash and blind manufacture in the city of Baltimore, where, during the late 1860's and early 1870's, the value of these manufactures tripled, and between 1870 and 1880, quadrupled. The Baltimore sash and blind industry was described thus in 1873:

> Thirteen Sash Factories, employing upwards of seven hundred hands, and manipulating $1,000,000 of capital, are at present in operation in this city. . . . The quality of the work done by our factories is fully up to the standard established in other cities. Offices, churches, and public buildings are fitted by the trade, in a style of taste and elegance unsurpassed elsewhere, and which has commanded the admiration of parties from abroad. Baltimore has great facilities in the way of securing lumber of the most available description, and upon the most advantageous terms. The factories engaged in the business, turn out all kinds of work, and offer as great inducements to purchasers as can be obtained in any other city in America. As large as the demand is for home consumption it by no means disposes of the material turned out by these establishments; and large quantities of Sash, Window Blinds, and general Finishings for buildings, are shipped to the Southern States, South America and the West Indies.

Baltimore was also the site of many other types of wood industries such as general carpentry and building, furniture making, packing boxes, and shipbuilding, but in 1880 the sash and blind manufactories ranked third among them in terms of the value of products made (but seventh in the number of hands employed.)

The firm was last listed as George O. Stevens & Co. in 1878. About this time D. G. Stevens left the business, and George O. Stevens operated under his name through 1891. This catalog thus dates from shortly after the dissolution of the partnership. Stevens utilized a variety of publications in which to advertise, including atlases, commercial city histories, and city directories, in which he invited prospective customers to send for "Catalogs & Prices."

Among the advertisements he placed in the directories was one in 1874 which announced that he handled "the Newest and Handsomest Patterns of Mantels in Statuary Marble, Italian Marble and Marbleized Slate." He was apparently an early dealer in marbleized slate, for in 1858 he submitted a marbleized mantel, made by the West Castleton Railroad and Slate Company of Vermont, to the annual exhibition of the Maryland Institute, where it was awarded a silver medal.

The 1891 Baltimore directory carried the notation that the firm was in liquidation. Between 1893 and 1896 Stevens appeared as manager of the "Geo. O. Stevens Doors & Window Co." That firm was not listed after 1896, although Stevens' name appeared in the directory for two more years.

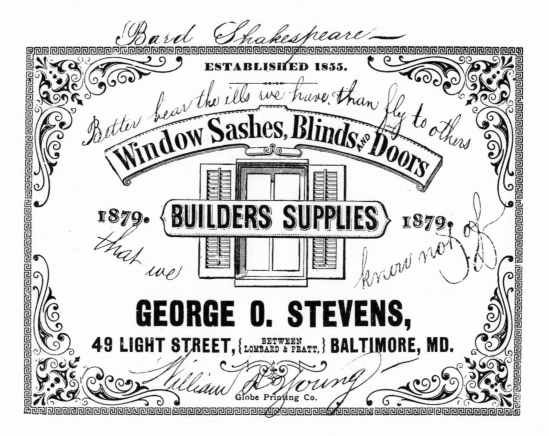

INDEX.

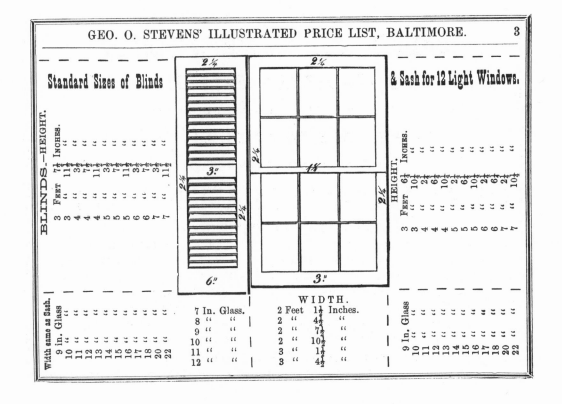

Standard Sizes of Blinds   & Sash for 12 Light Windows.

DOORS.
Raised Panels, Two Sides.

WIDTH		LENGTH		THICKNESS		
Ft.	In.	Ft.	In.	1¼	1⅜	1¾
2	0	6	0	$1.37	$1.52	
2	6	6	0	1.59	1.74	
2	4	6	4	1.61	1.76	
2	8	6	4	1.76	1.91	
2	0	6	6	1.45	1.60	
2	2	6	6	1.53	1.68	Seventy-five cents more than for 1⅜ Inch Doors.
2	4	6	6	1.63	1.78	
2	6	6	6	1.69	1.84	
2	8	6	6	1.76	1.91	
2	10	6	6	1.88	2.03	
3	0	6	6	1.98	2.13	
2	0	6	8	1.49	1.64	
2	2	6	8	1.55	1.70	
2	4	6	8	1.63	1.78	
2	6	6	8	1.73	1.88	
2	8	6	8	1.80	1.95	
2	10	6	8	1.90	2.05	
3	0	6	8	2.02	2.17	

DOORS.
Raised Panels, Two Sides.

WIDTH		LENGTH		THICKNESS		
Ft.	In.	Ft.	In.	1¼	1⅜	1¾
2	0	6	10	$1.50	$1.65	
2	6	6	10	1.76	1.91	
2	8	6	10	1.88	2.03	
2	10	6	10	1.98	2.13	
3	0	6	10	2.05	2.20	
2	0	7	0	1.53	1.68	
2	6	7	0	1.80	1.95	
2	8	7	0	1.88	2.03	Seventy-five cents more than for 1⅜ Inch Doors.
2	10	7	0	1.98	2.13	
3	0	7	0	2.07	2.22	
2	6	7	6	1.88	2.03	
2	8	7	6	1.99	2.14	
2	10	7	6	2.10	2.25	
3	0	7	6		2.65	
2	10	8	0		2.75	
3	0	8	0		3.00	

EXTRAS.

Extra for O. G. solid Moulded Doors, each, 15 cents.
" " Moulding per side, 1¼ inch Doors, 25 "
" "   "   " 1⅜ " " 33 "
" "   "   " 1¾ " " 40 "
Less for second quality, 20 cents.
" " third " 30 "
Sash Doors, 25 cts extra. With Cir. Top Glass, 60 cts ex

CULL DOORS.

2	6	x	6	6,	$1.15	3	0	x	6	6,	$1.40
2	8	x	6	8,	1.25	2	10	x	6	10,	1.40
2	10	x	6	6,	1.35	3	0	x	7	0,	1.45

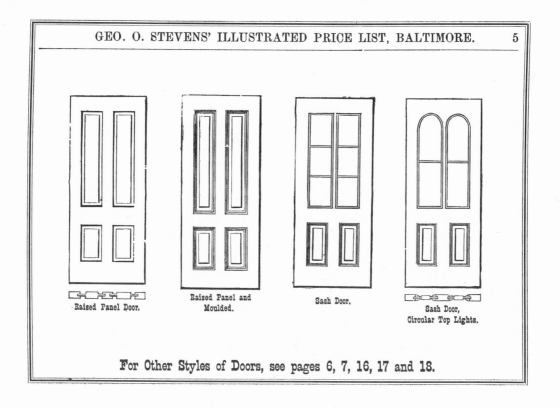

Raised Panel Door. Raised Panel and Moulded. Sash Door. Sash Door, Circular Top Lights.

For Other Styles of Doors, see pages 6, 7, 16, 17 and 18.

FRONT DOORS.

THE PRICES GIVEN BELOW ARE FOR WHITE PINE
DOORS, OF BEST QUALITY, HAVING ON ONE
SIDE HEAVY RAISED MOULDING AND
CIRCULAR HEAD PANELS, AND
ON OTHER SIDE FLUSH MOULDINGS AND SQUARE
PANELS LIKE CUT B.

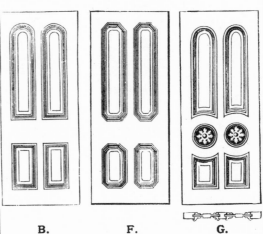

B.   F.   G.

STOCK SIZES.	THICKNESS.	
	$1\frac{3}{8}$	$1\frac{3}{4}$
2 6 x 6 6	$4.25	$4.75
2 8 x 6 8	4.60	5.10
2 10 x 6 10	4.90	5.50
3 0 x 7 0	5.00	5.75
2 10 x 6 6	4.90	5.50
3 0 x 6 6	4.90	5.75

Add for Extra Heavy Raised Mouldings from $1.50
     to $2.50.
  "   Vestibule Doors, 50 cents to $1.50.
Add to above prices for Pattern F, 75 cents.
  "   "   "   "   " G, 4.00.

Black Walnut, Ash, Cherry, Chestnut,
Maple, Butternut and Mahogany Doors,
both Solid and Veneered, furnished to
Order.

For other Styles of Front Doors, see pages 7, 17, 18 and 44.

FRONT DOORS.

OF BEST QUALITY WHITE PINE HAVING ON ONE SIDE
HEAVY RAISED MOULDING AND CIRCULAR
HEAD PANELS, AND ON THE OTHER SIDE
FLUSH MOULDINGS AND SQUARE
PANELS LIKE CUT I.

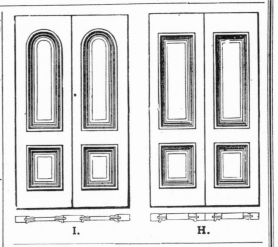

I.   H.

SIZES. IN PAIRS.	THICKNESS.	
	$1\frac{3}{8}$ Inch.	$1\frac{3}{4}$ Inch.
4 0 x 7 0	$ 9.00	$10.00
4 4 x 7 0	9.50	10.50
4 0 x 7 6	10.00	11.00
4 4 x 7 6	10.50	11.50
5 0 x 7 6	12.00	13.00
4 6 x 8 0	12.00	13.00
5 0 x 8 0	13.00	14.00

Add for Extra Heavy Raised Mouldings from
     $1.50 to $2.50.
Add for Vestibule Doors, made for Glass Panels,
     50 cts. to $1.50.
Deduct from above for Pattern H, $1.25.

Black Walnut and other Hard-wood Front Doors
made to order and Designs furnished if desired.—See
pages 44, 64, 65 and 66.
Enameled, Engraved or other Fancy Lights of single
or double thick Glass or of French Plate for Door Panels,
&c., of New and Old Designs, furnished to order.

For other Styles of Double Front Doors, see pages 17, 18, 64, 65 and 66.

WINDOW SASHES.
12 Light Windows.

SIZE OF GLASS	WIDTH Ft. In.	LENG'H Ft. In.	UNGLAZED. 1¼ Plain.	1⅜ Plain.	PRIMED & GLAZED. 1¼ Plain.	1⅜ Plain.
7x 9	2 1½	3 6¼	45	60	96	1.12
8x10	2 4½	3 10¼	48	70	1.07	1.22
8x12	2 4½	4 6¼	60	80	1.25	1.41
9x11	2 7½	4 2¼	60	80	1.30	1.43
9x12	2 7½	4 6¼	60	80	1.35	1.48
9x13	2 7½	4 10¼	65	85	1.44	1.59
9x14	2 7½	5 2¼	65	85	1.56	1.70
9x15	2 7½	5 6¼	70	90	1.67	1.83
9x16	2 7½	5 10¼	75	95	1.76	1.97
9x18	2 7½	6 6¼	95	1.15	2.16	2.36
10x12	2 10½	4 6¼	62	82	1.43	1.63
10x13	2 10½	4 10¼	70	90	1.61	1.88
10x14	2 10½	5 2¼	70	90	1.61	1.88
10x15	2 10½	5 6¼	75	95	1.75	2.00
10x16	2 10½	5 10¼	80	1.00	2.00	2.30
10x18	2 10½	6 6¼	....	1.20	....	2.60
10x20	2 10½	7 2¼	....	1.30	....	2.80
12x14	3 4½	5 2¼	....	1.10	....	2.50
12x16	3 4½	5 10¼	....	1.25	....	2.65
12x18	3 4½	6 6¼	....	1.35	....	2.70
12x20	3 4½	7 2¼	....	1.40	....	3.00
12x24	3 4½	8 6¼	....	1.75	....	3.30

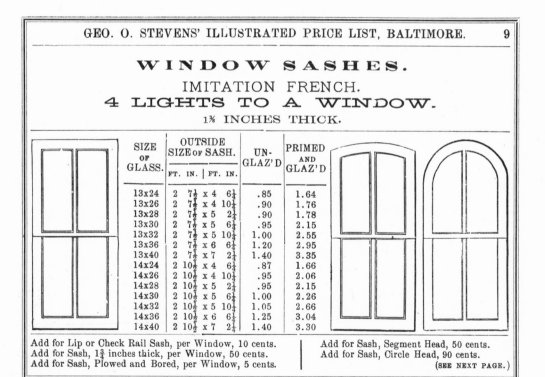

OVALO SASH MOULDING.

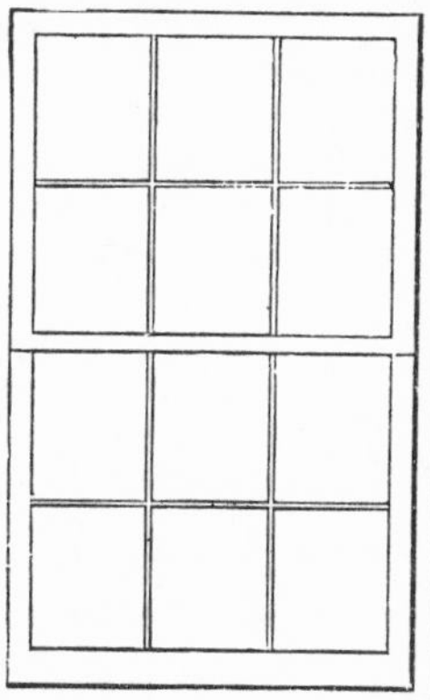

Add for Lip or Check Rail Sash, per Window, 10 cents.

Add for Sash, 1¾ thick, per Window 50 cts.

Add for Sash plowed and bored, per Window, 5 cents.

Add for Segment Head, per Window, 50 cents.

Add for Circle Head, per Window, 90 cts.

For Other Styles, see pages 9, 10, 11, 19 and 20.

WINDOW SASHES.
IMITATION FRENCH.
4 LIGHTS TO A WINDOW.
1⅜ INCHES THICK.

SIZE OF GLASS.	OUTSIDE SIZE OF SASH. FT. IN.	FT. IN.	UN-GLAZ'D	PRIMED AND GLAZ'D
13x24	2 7½ x 4	6¼	.85	1.64
13x26	2 7½ x 4	10¼	.90	1.76
13x28	2 7½ x 5	2¼	.90	1.78
13x30	2 7½ x 5	6¼	.95	2.15
13x32	2 7½ x 5	10¼	1.00	2.55
13x36	2 7½ x 6	6¼	1.20	2.95
13x40	2 7½ x 7	2¼	1.40	3.35
14x24	2 10½ x 4	6¼	.87	1.66
14x26	2 10½ x 4	10¼	.95	2.06
14x28	2 10½ x 5	2¼	.95	2.15
14x30	2 10½ x 5	6¼	1.00	2.26
14x32	2 10½ x 5	10¼	1.05	2.66
14x36	2 10½ x 6	6¼	1.25	3.04
14x40	2 10½ x 7	2¼	1.40	3.30

Add for Lip or Check Rail Sash, per Window, 10 cents.
Add for Sash, 1¾ inches thick, per Window, 50 cents.
Add for Sash, Plowed and Bored, per Window, 5 cents.

Add for Sash, Segment Head, 50 cents.
Add for Sash, Circle Head, 90 cents.

(SEE NEXT PAGE.)

WINDOW SASHES.

IMITATION FRENCH.

8 LIGHTS TO A WINDOW.

1⅜ INCHES THICK.

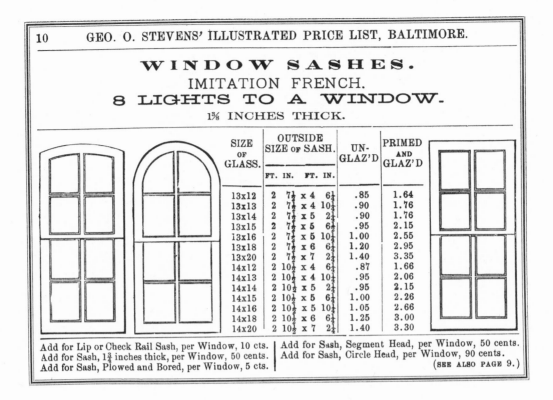

SIZE OF GLASS.	OUTSIDE SIZE OF SASH. FT. IN. FT. IN.	UN-GLAZ'D	PRIMED AND GLAZ'D
13x12	2 7½ x 4 6¼	.85	1.64
13x13	2 7½ x 4 10¼	.90	1.76
13x14	2 7½ x 5 2¼	.90	1.76
13x15	2 7½ x 5 6½	.95	2.15
13x16	2 7½ x 5 10¼	1.00	2.55
13x18	2 7½ x 6 6¼	1.20	2.95
13x20	2 7½ x 7 2¼	1.40	3.35
14x12	2 10½ x 4 6¼	.87	1.66
14x13	2 10½ x 4 10¼	.95	2.06
14x14	2 10½ x 5 2¼	.95	2.15
14x15	2 10½ x 5 6¼	1.00	2.26
14x16	2 10½ x 5 10¼	1.05	2.66
14x18	2 10½ x 6 6¼	1.25	3.00
14x20	2 10½ x 7 2¼	1.40	3.30

Add for Lip or Check Rail Sash, per Window, 10 cts.
Add for Sash, 1¾ inches thick, per Window, 50 cents.
Add for Sash, Plowed and Bored, per Window, 5 cts.

Add for Sash, Segment Head, per Window, 50 cents.
Add for Sash, Circle Head, per Window, 90 cents.

(SEE ALSO PAGE 9.)

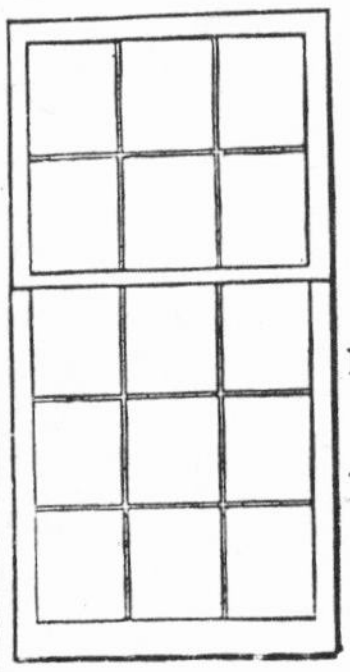

SASHES.

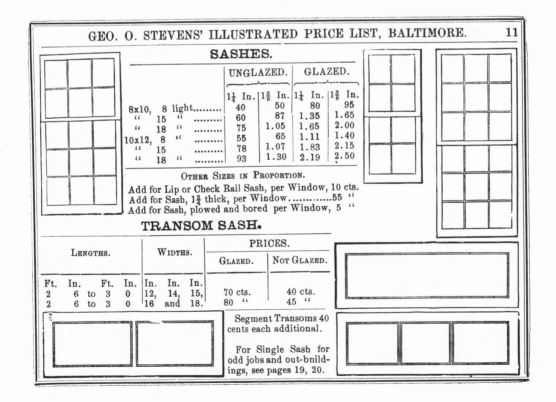

	UNGLAZED. 1¼ In.	UNGLAZED. 1⅜ In.	GLAZED. 1¼ In.	GLAZED. 1⅜ In.
8x10, 8 light.........	40	50	80	95
" 15 "	60	87	1.35	1.65
" 18 "	75	1.05	1.65	2.00
10x12, 8 "	55	65	1.11	1.40
" 15	78	1.07	1.83	2.15
" 18 "	93	1.30	2.19	2.50

OTHER SIZES IN PROPORTION.

Add for Lip or Check Rail Sash, per Window, 10 cts.
Add for Sash, 1¾ thick, per Window.............55 "
Add for Sash, plowed and bored per Window, 5 "

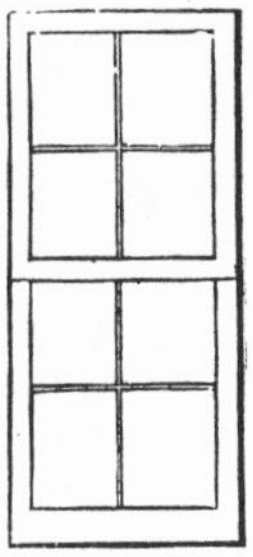

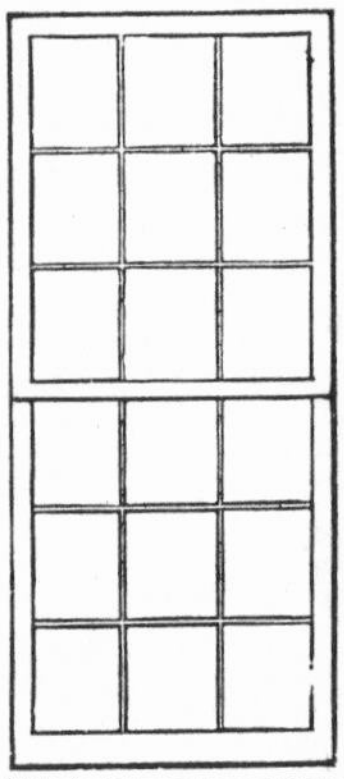

TRANSOM SASH.

LENGTHS. Ft.	In.		Ft.	In.	WIDTHS. In.	In.	In.	PRICES. GLAZED.	PRICES. NOT GLAZED.
2	6	to	3	0	12,	14,	15,	70 cts.	40 cts.
2	6	to	3	0	16	and	18.	80 "	45 "

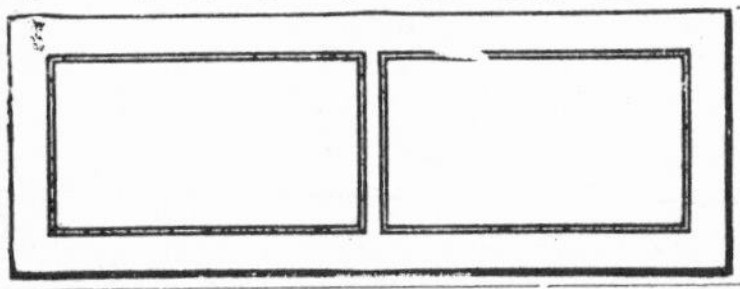

Segment Transoms 40 cents each additional.

For Single Sash for odd jobs and out-buildings, see pages 19, 20.

OUTSIDE WINDOW BLINDS TO SUIT 12 LIGHT WINDOWS.

For Blinds of 1⅜ inch in thickness, add for sizes 10x15 and under, 20 cents. Add for Sizes 10x16 to 12x24, 50 cents.

SIZE OF GLASS.	WIDTH. Ft. In.	LEN'TH Ft. In.	PRICE PER PAIR. 1 3-16 In
7 x 9	2 1½	3 7½	$1.25
8 x 10	2 4½	3 11½	1.25
8 x 12	2 4½	4 7½	1.50
9 x 11	2 7½	4 3½	1.50
9 x 12	2 7½	4 7½	1.50
9 x 13	2 7½	4 11½	1.65
9 x 14	2 7½	5 3½	1.65
9 x 15	2 7½	5 7½	1.75
9 x 16	2 7½	5 11½	1.75
9 x 18	2 7½	6 7½	2.00
10 x 12	2 10½	4 7½	1.50
10 x 13	2 10½	4 11½	1.70
10 x 14	2 10½	5 3½	1.70
10 x 15	2 10½	5 7½	1.75
10 x 16	2 10½	5 11½	1.75
10 x 18	2 10½	6 7½	2.15
10 x 20	2 10½	7 3½	2.30
12 x 14	3 4½	5 3½	1.85
12 x 16	3 4½	5 11½	2.00
12 x 18	3 4½	6 7½	2.40
12 x 20	3 4½	7 3½	2.60
12 x 24	3 4½	8 7½	3.10

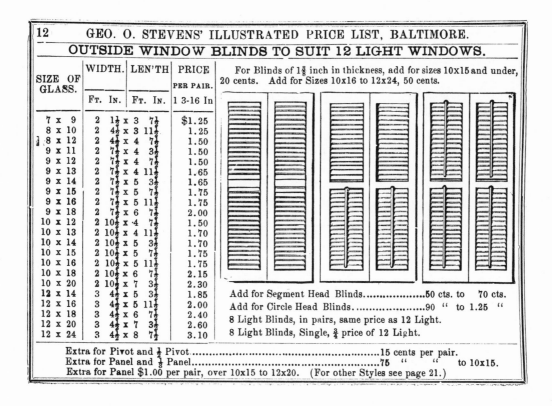

Add for Segment Head Blinds....................50 cts. to 70 cts.
Add for Circle Head Blinds.......................90 " to 1.25 "
8 Light Blinds, in pairs, same price as 12 Light.
8 Light Blinds, Single, ¾ price of 12 Light.

Extra for Pivot and ½ Pivot...15 cents per pair.
Extra for Panel and ⅓ Panel...75 " " to 10x15.
Extra for Panel $1.00 per pair, over 10x15 to 12x20. (For other Styles see page 21.)

FOUR-FOLD INSIDE SHUTTERS.

Measuring height of window, ordinary width,
  ⅞ inch thick, 60 cents per linear foot.
  70 cents a foot if made of 1¼ inch stuff.
  80 cents a foot if made of 1½ inch stuff.
1.75 per Window, extra, for Circle Head.
1.00 per Window, extra, for Segment Head.

The above price is for Pine. Of hard wood, such as Cherry, Ash, Maple or Black Walnut, we charge about double the price of Pine. We make Inside Blinds that are not excelled, either in workmanship or style, in this market.

In ordering Inside Shutters, give the full *length* and *width* of Shutters over all when Rabbetted, and the *height* from bottom to the centre of the Meeting Rail.

If they are intended to fold back into boxes, state the width of the boxes, and whether *straight* or *splayed*.

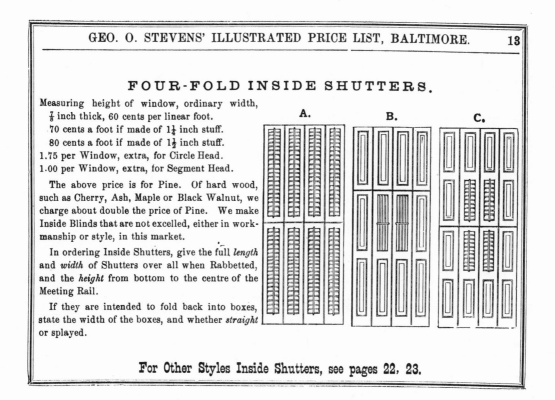

For Other Styles Inside Shutters, see pages 22, 23.

Window Frames made of 1½ inch White Pine, to suit 12 Light Windows.

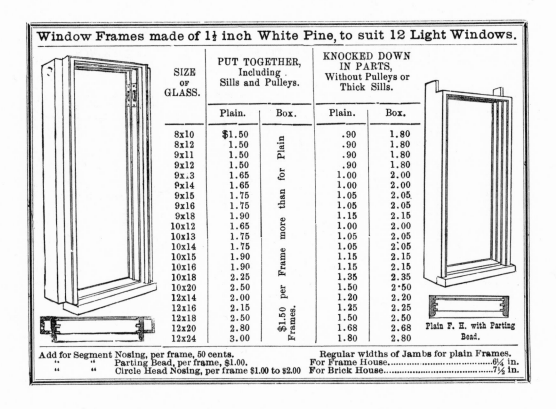

SIZE OF GLASS.	PUT TOGETHER, Including Sills and Pulleys.		KNOCKED DOWN IN PARTS, Without Pulleys or Thick Sills.	
	Plain.	Box.	Plain.	Box.
8x10	$1.50		.90	1.80
8x12	1.50		.90	1.80
9x11	1.50		.90	1.80
9x12	1.50		.90	1.80
9x13	1.65		1.00	2.00
9x14	1.65		1.00	2.00
9x15	1.75		1.05	2.05
9x16	1.75		1.05	2.05
9x18	1.90	$1.50 per Frame more than for Plain Frames.	1.15	2.15
10x12	1.65		1.00	2.00
10x13	1.75		1.05	2.05
10x14	1.75		1.05	2.05
10x15	1.90		1.15	2.15
10x16	1.90		1.15	2.15
10x18	2.25		1.35	2.35
10x20	2.50		1.50	2.50
12x14	2.00		1.20	2.20
12x16	2.15		1.25	2.25
12x18	2.50		1.50	2.50
12x20	2.80		1.68	2.68
12x24	3.00		1.80	2.80

Plain F. H. with Parting Bead.

Add for Segment Nosing, per frame, 50 cents.
" " Parting Bead, per frame, $1.00.
" " Circle Head Nosing, per frame $1.00 to $2.00

Regular widths of Jambs for plain Frames.
For Frame House..6¼ in.
For Brick House..7½ in.

Door Frames, made of 1½ In. White Pine, for Doors 3x7 Feet and Under.

Put together, Plain, $2.25. Put together, Transom, $2 50. Knock-down, Plain, $1.50, Knock-down, Transom, $1.70, without Sills. Add for Side-light and Transom Frames, $3.00 to $4.00.

For Other Patterns of Frames, see pages 5, 14 and 24.

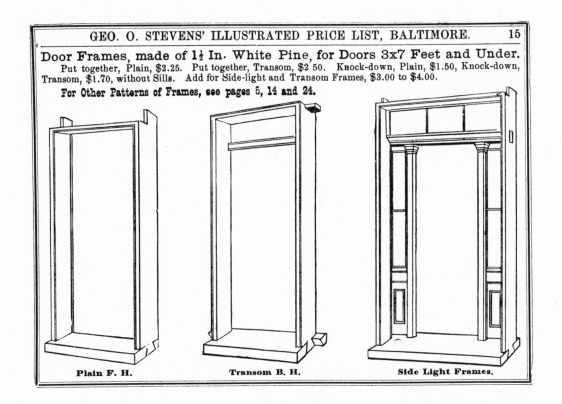

Plain F. H.   **Transom B. H.**   **Side Light Frames.**

FRONT DOORS.   INSIDE DOORS.

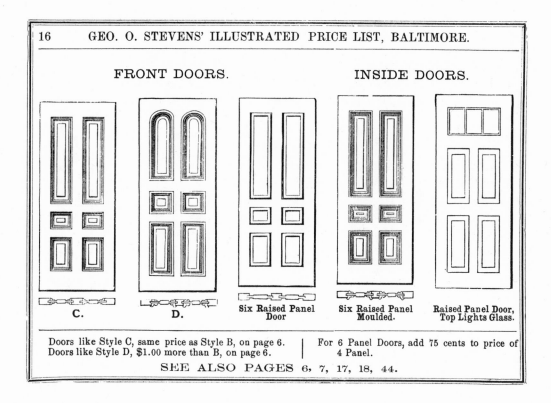

C.   D.   Six Raised Panel Door   Six Raised Panel Moulded.   Raised Panel Door, Top Lights Glass.

Doors like Style C, same price as Style B, on page 6.   For 6 Panel Doors, add 75 cents to price of
Doors like Style D, $1.00 more than B, on page 6.   4 Panel.

SEE ALSO PAGES 6, 7, 17, 18, 44.

FRONT DOORS IN PAIRS.

SEE ALSO PAGES 7, 18, 64, 65, 66.

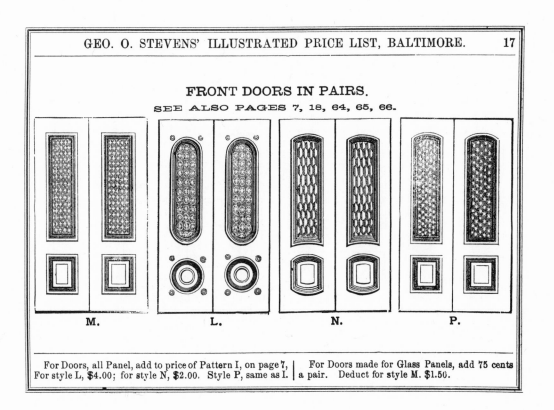

M.   L.   N.   P.

For Doors, all Panel, add to price of Pattern I, on page 7,   For Doors made for Glass Panels, add 75 cents
For style L, $4.00; for style N, $2.00. Style P, same as I.   a pair.   Deduct for style M. $1.50.

FRONT DOORS IN PAIRS.

SEE ALSO PAGES 7, 17, 64, 65, 66.

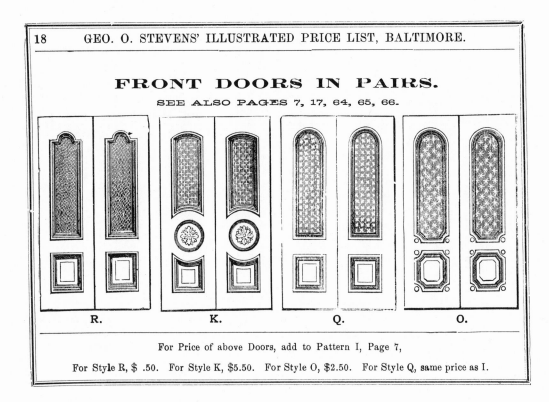

R.   **K.**   **Q.**   **O.**

For Price of above Doors, add to Pattern I, Page 7,

For Style R, $ .50.   For Style K, $5.50.   For Style O, $2.50.   For Style Q, same price as I.

---

24 Light.   20 Lights.   9 Lights.   6 Lights.   4 Lights.

6 Lights.   4 Lights.

16 Lights.   10 Lights.

8 Lights.

Unglazed Four, Six, Eight, Nine and Ten Light Windows, are same price as Twelve Light Windows. Sixteen Light are twice price of Twelve Light. Twenty Light are $2\frac{1}{2}$ times price of Twelve Light. Twenty-four Light are three times price of Twelve Light Windows.

Glazing, per doz. Lights, same price as charged for Twelve Light Windows.

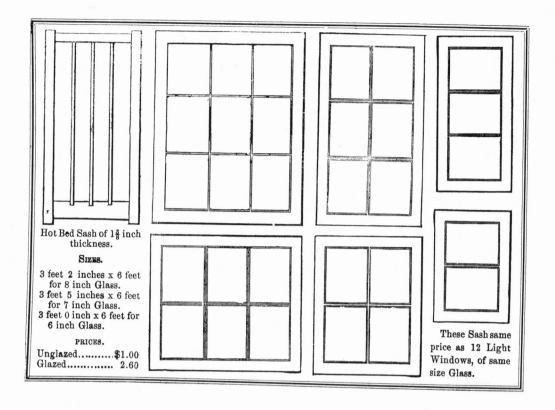

Hot Bed Sash of 1⅜ inch
thickness.

SIZES.

3 feet 2 inches x 6 feet
for 8 inch Glass.
3 feet 5 inches x 6 feet
for 7 inch Glass.
3 feet 0 inch x 6 feet for
6 inch Glass.

PRICES.

Unglazed..........$1.00
Glazed.............. 2.60

These Sash same
price as 12 Light
Windows, of same
size Glass.

OUTSIDE WINDOW BLINDS AND SHUTTERS.

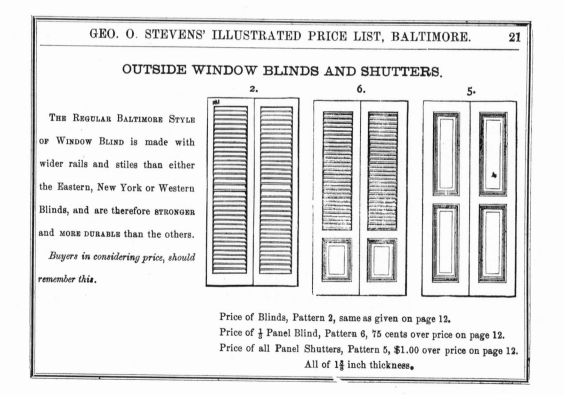

THE REGULAR BALTIMORE STYLE OF WINDOW BLIND is made with wider rails and stiles than either the Eastern, New York or Western Blinds, and are therefore STRONGER and MORE DURABLE than the others.

Buyers in considering price, should remember this.

Price of Blinds, Pattern 2, same as given on page 12.
Price of ⅓ Panel Blind, Pattern 6, 75 cents over price on page 12.
Price of all Panel Shutters, Pattern 5, $1.00 over price on page 12.
All of 1⅜ inch thickness.

INSIDE BLINDS AND SHUTTERS.

SEE ALSO PAGES 13 AND 23.

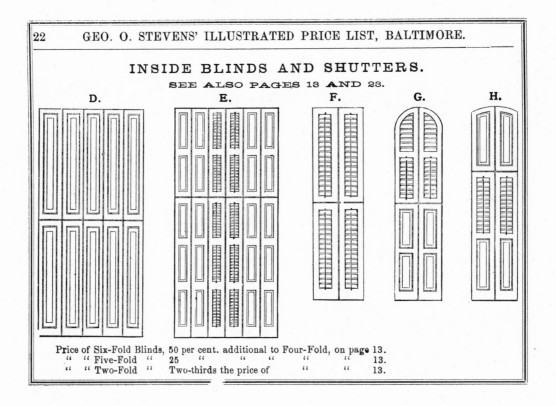

D.   E.   F.   G.   H.

Price of Six-Fold Blinds, 50 per cent. additional to Four-Fold, on page 13.
   "   " Five-Fold   "   25   "   "   "   "   "   13.
   "   " Two-Fold   "   Two-thirds the price of   "   "   13.

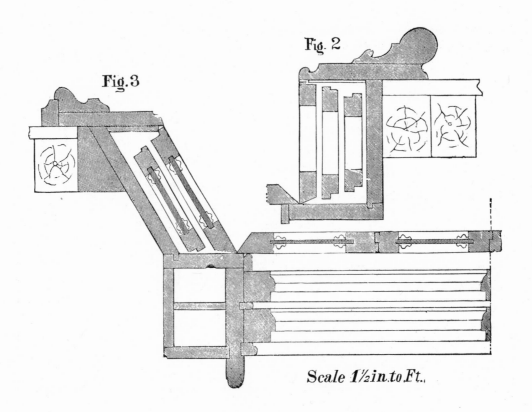

Fig. 3

Fig. 2

Scale 1½ in. to Ft.,

WINDOW FRAMES.

For Hood Frames, add $2.00 to same size Box Frames. See p. 14.

Dormer Window Frame.

Segment Head, Box Frame.   Circle Head, Box Frame.   Hood Frame.

SEE ALSO PAGES 14, 15, 25.

WINDOW FRAMES.   # DOOR JAMBS AND FRAME.

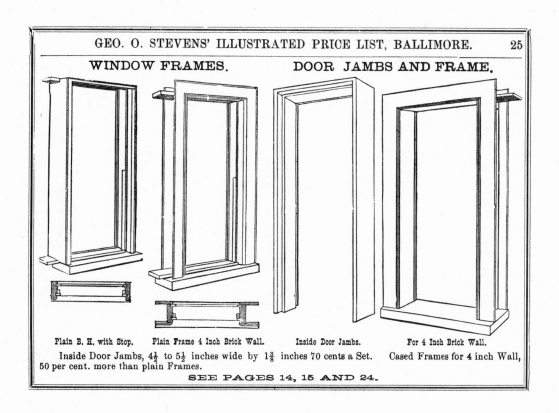

Plain B. H. with Stop.   Plain Frame 4 Inch Brick Wall.   Inside Door Jambs.   For 4 Inch Brick Wall.

Inside Door Jambs, $4\frac{1}{2}$ to $5\frac{1}{2}$ inches wide by $1\frac{3}{8}$ inches 70 cents a Set.   Cased Frames for 4 inch Wall,
50 per cent. more than plain Frames.

SEE PAGES 14, 15 AND 24.

STORE DOORS.

Heavy Raised Mouldings Outside, with Sash Rabbetted on and Shutters Fitted.

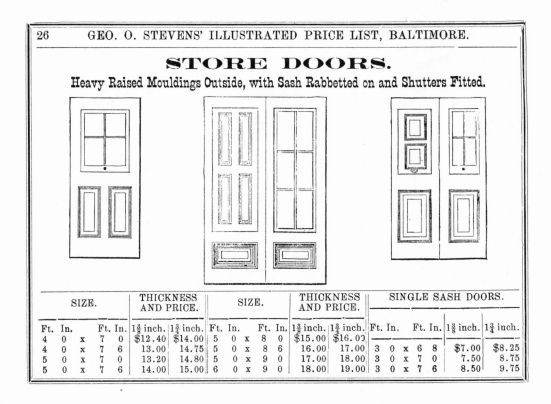

SIZE.				THICKNESS AND PRICE.		SIZE.				THICKNESS AND PRICE.		SINGLE SASH DOORS.			
Ft.	In.		Ft.	In.	$1\frac{3}{8}$ inch.	$1\frac{3}{4}$ inch.	Ft.	In.		Ft.	In.	$1\frac{3}{8}$ inch.	$1\frac{3}{4}$ inch.	Ft.	In.	Ft.	In.	$1\frac{3}{8}$ inch.	$1\frac{3}{4}$ inch.
4	0	x	7	0	$12.40	$14.00	5	0	x	8	0	$15.00	$16.00						
4	0	x	7	6	13.00	14.75	5	0	x	8	6	16.00	17.00	3	0	x	6	8	$7.00	$8.25
5	0	x	7	0	13.20	14.80	5	0	x	9	0	17.00	18.00	3	0	x	7	0	7.50	8.75
5	0	x	7	6	14.00	15.00	6	0	x	9	0	18.00	19.00	3	0	x	7	6	8.50	9.75

ROUND AND SQUARE SASH WEIGHTS.

Northup's Patent Window Spring, Sash Locks and Supporter.

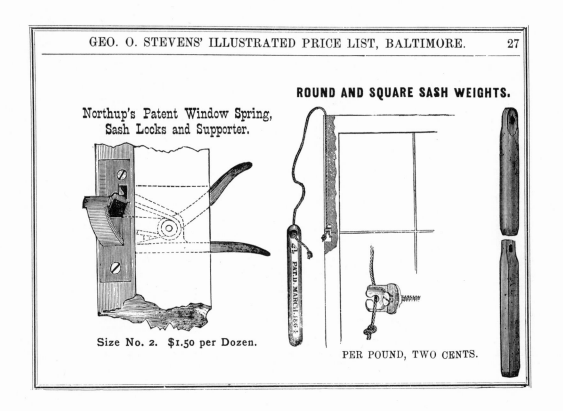

Size No. 2. $1.50 per Dozen.

PER POUND, TWO CENTS.

TABLE OF WEIGHTS OF SASH, DOORS AND BLINDS.

SASH AND BLINDS.

12 Light Win'ds.	8 Light Win'ds.	4 Light Win'ds.	1¼ inch. Ungl'd.	1¼ inch. Glazed.	1⅜ inch. Ungl'd.	1⅜ inch. Glazed.	Blinds. pr. p'r.
8x10	12x10	12x20	7 lbs	15 lbs	8½ lbs	17½ lbs	13 lbs
8x12	12x12	12x24	8	18	9	19	15½
9x11	13x11	13x22	8	19	9	18½	16
9x12	13x12	13x24	8½	20	9½	23	16½
9x13	13x13	13x26	9	21½	10	24	17
9x14	13x14	13x28	9½	23	10½	25	18
9x15	13x15	13x30	10	24	11	27	19
9x16	13x16	13x32	10½	25	11½	28	19½
9x18	13x18	13x36	11	28	12	31	22
10x12	14x12	14x24	8½	21	10	25	18
10x13	14x13	14x26	9	23	10½	26	19
10x14	14x14	14x28	9½	25	11	27	19½
10x15	14x15	14x30	10	26	11½	28½	20
10x16	14x16	14x32	11	27	12½	30	20½
10x18	14x18	14x36	12	28	13½	33	22
10x20	14x20	14x40	13	30	14½	35	24
12x14			10½	28	13	30	26
12x16			11	30	13½	34	28
12x18			11½	32	14	36	31
12x20			12	34	15½	40	34
12x24			15½	38	17	46	40

DOORS.

Sizes.	1¼ in. Pl.	1⅜ in. Pl	Moulded. 1⅜ inch.	Moulded. 1¾ inch.
2 6x6 6	33 lbs.	37 lbs.	38 lbs.	46 lbs.
2 8x6 8	35	40	41	50
2 10x6 10	37	42	44	54
3 0x7 0	39	46	48	59
3 0x7 6	47	54	56	65
3 0x8 0	53	56	58	70

WOOD MANTELS.

Pages	Pattern.	White Pine.	Walnut.
46, 47, 48.	776	$4.00	$ 9.00
	777	4.50	11.00
	778	2.25	
	785	4.25	12.00
	779	2.80	

BRACKET SHELVES.

Pages	Pattern.	White Pine.	Walnut.
46 and 47.	780	$1.50	$3.75
	781	1.50	3.75
	786	1.25	3.50
	787	1.25	3.50

SAWED BALUSTRADE.

OF WHITE PINE, ⅞ IN. THICK, 6 IN. WIDE AND 26 IN. LONG.

(PAGES 52 AND 53.)

681, 684 and 687.......................................Each 12 cents.
682, 691.. " 18 "
690, 692, 693, 694...................................... " 14 "

HAND RAILS, (Black Wal.)

Pattern.		
Page 39–528	3 x 1⅞	12 cts.
872	3½ x 1⅞	14 "
873	3 x 2¼	14 "
	3½ x 2¼	16 "
	4 x 2¼	18 "
	4½ x 2½	23 "
	5 x 2½	25 "

WINDOW CAPS.

(Ordinary Width.)

Pattern.	
Page 48–702	4.00
703	5 00
708	2 00
853	1.25
854	1.00

VERGE BOARDS.

(PAGES 52 AND 53.)

Pattern.	Per Ft.	Size.	Pattern.	Per Ft.	Size.
647	14c	1x9	653	14c	1x 9
648	15c	1x9	657	24c	2x12
649	12c	1x9			

PORCH BRACKETS.

(PAGES 52 AND 53.)

No. 674	24x24x1½	$1 00
" 675	30x30x3	2 25
" 678	30x24x2	1 50
	24x12x2	56
" 660—	26x12x4	1 00
	24x11x3	90
	20x10x2	60
" 655—	16x16x2	85
	20x20x1½	90
" 679	30x24x2	1 75
" 680	36x30x3	3 00
	48x24x2	3 00

SAWED MOULDING,

Pine or Poplar.

(PAGE 59.)

	Sizes.	Per Ft.		Sizes.	Per Ft.
624to642,	1½x ⅞	.11	624to642,	2¼x1⅜	.17
	1¾x1½	.14		3 x1¾	.20
	1½x1¼	.14		3½x2¼	.23
	2 x1⅜	.15		4 x3	.30
	2¼x1⅜	.16			

PEW CAPS, (Black Walnut.)

Pattern.	
Page 39—238, A	6 cts.
238	11 "
243	6 "

ORNAMENTAL GLASS.

As an aid to customers in making selections of ORNAMENTAL GLASS, I have introduced into my Price List several pages of desirable designs. The patterns shown on pages 60, 61, 62, 63, with prices given below, being cut on "*Double Thick*" *Imported Glass*, will always retain their handsome appearance, and can be depended upon for durability and strength. In the long run this Glass is really cheaper than other kinds, and deserves to be recommended before all other kinds, for *Doors, Side Lights, Transoms*, and for all windows where ornamental lights are required.

The same style of work is done on *Plate Glass* to order. *Stained, Tinted,* or *Enameled Glass*, for Church or other windows, furnished at reasonable prices to order.

Ordinary French and *American Glass, of Single* and *Double Thickness,* and *Plate Glass*, supplied at market rates.

Prices of Ornamental Cut Glass per Square Foot. (See designs on Pages 60, 61, 62, 63.)

No. 49	$1.50	No. 141	$1.70	No. 595	$2.25
" 50	1.00	" 269	1.35	" 607	1.25
" 53	1.10	" 524	1.00	" 610	1.00
" 63	1.30	" 532	1.15	" 614	1.70
" 64	1.50	" 563	1.70	" 618	1.00
" 76	1.70	" 574	1.75	" 619	1.00
" 78	1.50	" 576	1.25	" 620	1.00
" 140	1.70	" 593	4.00	" 628	1.00

BRACKETS.

PAGE.	PATTERN.		PRICE.
54 and 55	857	2 feet x 2 feet x 1½ in	$1.20
	860	2 feet x 22 in. x 2 in	1.40
	864	18 in. x 24 in. x 1½ in	1.00
	867	18 in. x 18 in. x 1½ in	.75
	866	16 in. x 16 in. x 1½ in	.55
		10 in. x 12 in. x 1½ in	.30
55	865	30 in. x 30 in. x 1¾ in	2.00
55 and 56.	858	13 in. x 16 in. x 4 in	.60
	861	14 in. x 18 in. x 4 in	.75
	862	14 in. x 9 in. x 3 in	.45
	869	16 in. x 16 in. x 3 in	.60
55 and 56.	868	18 in. x 18 in. x 5 in	.90
	870	16 in. x 14 in. x 4 in	.60
		12 in. x 12 in. x 3 in	.40
	859	14 in. x 22 in. x 6 in	1.50
55	863	8 in. x 12 in. x 2 in	.23
		10 in. x 12 in. x 3 in	.30
		10 in. x 14 in. x 3 in	.36
56	871	10 in. x 17 x 2	.40
		12 in. x 22 x 2½ in	.63
	597	12 in. x 21 in. x 5 in	1 20
	615	12 in. x 18 in. x 4 in	.70
	608	10 in. x 16 in. x 4 in	.56
	609	9 in. x 18 in. x 4 in	.68
	611	12 in. x 20 in. x 5 in	1.20
	621	14 in. x 16 in. x 4 in	.75
	622	18 in. x 18 in. x 5 in	1.30

PAGE.	PATTERN.		PRICE.
56	623	7 in. x 11 in. x 4 in	.56
	619	8 in. x 12 in. x 4 in	.65
	610	10 in. x 16 in. x 2½ in	.30
		12 in. x 18 in. x 3 in	.40
		10 in. x 12 in. x 2 in	.25

STAIR BRACKETS.

PAGE.	PATTERN.	
56	590	
	591	8 cents each.
	593	
	595	

PEW ENDS.

PAGE.	PATTERN.	POPLAR.		BLACK WALNUT.	
		1 1-2 in.	2 in.	1 1-2 in.	2 in.
57	733	1.35	1.60	2.50	3.00
	734	1.35	1.60	2.50	3.00
	735	1.35	1.60	2.50	3.00
	736	1.35	1.60	2.50	3.00
	737	3.15	3.50	5.00	5.50
	738	1.35	1.55	2.50	3.00

PEW ARMS.

PAGE.	PATTERN.	SAWED BUT UNFINISHED.	FINISHED COMPLETE.
57	4 Poplar,	.35	.80
	Blk Walnut,	.60	$1.15

Prices of Moulding per 100 Linear Feet.

No.	Price.	No.	Price.
Page 67—56	.75	Page 68—53	.60
57	.60	405	.60
58	.60	818	2.40
83	.90	Page 69—41	2.70
168	1.80	45	.75
173	1.80	60	.85
187	1.95	66	3.00
188 4 in x $\frac{7}{8}$ in	2.40	71	.90
188 5 in. x $\frac{7}{8}$	3.00	76	3 90
397	.70	80	.95
398	.70	93	1.50
400	.90	119	1.75
406	.45	167	1.20
512	.70	404	.60
Page 68—8 4 x $\frac{7}{8}$	2.40	Page 70—84	.75
8 5 x $\frac{7}{8}$	3.00	85	.70
8 6 x $\frac{7}{8}$	3.60	393	2.25
8 6 x $1\frac{1}{4}$	4.50	790	1.50
8 6 x $1\frac{1}{2}$	5.40	791	1.20
8 7 x $1\frac{1}{2}$	6.30	799	.90
8 8 x $1\frac{1}{2}$	7.20	803 4 x $1\frac{1}{4}$	3.00
8 $8\frac{3}{4}$ x $1\frac{3}{4}$	10.50	803 $4\frac{3}{4}$ x $1\frac{1}{2}$	4.50
8 $9\frac{1}{4}$ x $1\frac{3}{4}$	12.00	821	1.65
9	2.10	829 $2\frac{1}{2}$ x $1\frac{1}{4}$	1.80
14	2.85	829 $2\frac{5}{8}$ x $1\frac{3}{4}$	3.00
32	2.30	829 $2\frac{7}{8}$ x $1\frac{3}{4}$	3.60
51	1.15		

DIRECTIONS FOR ORDERING HAND RAILS.

1st.   Give size and pattern of rail wanted, and state whether the rail is at the right or left hand when ascending stairs.

2d.   Give the number and width of steps, and number and height of risers.

3d.   Give the diameter of well hole or cylinder in the clear.

4th.   Give the length of straight rails for floor landings above first-story.

5th.   To illustrate and explain above directions, it is advisable to accompany them with a ground plan of stairs, (a rough one will answer.

6th.   For WINDING STAIRS it is *always* necessary to give a plan of stairs showing, besides the above particulars, the position of steps and risers in the cylinder or string board.

N. B.   The variation in stairs is so great that it is impracticable to publish a Price List for Worked Hand Rails complete, but statements of their cost (always inclusive of Newel Caps and Hand Rail Screws) are furnished promptly upon application by letter or otherwise.

Outside Window Blinds

(WITH TRIMMINGS.)

FITTED AND PAINTED.

Although in the New York and Eastern Markets it has been long the custom for Dealers and Manufacturers to sell Outside Window Blinds, fitted to size, with Hinges and Fastenings applied, painted and ready for hanging, it has not been customary to do so in this Market.   I propose hereafter to furnish Blinds, painted in the best manner, and fitted with the most approved hinges and fastenings.   Unless otherwise ordered I shall use on Blinds the Elbow Hinges and the Screw Blind Fasts, as shown on page 35.

The additional cost of Hardware and Painting will be as follows:

Blinds not over 3 feet wide and 4 feet long ....$1.30 a pair.
  "   "   "   "   over 4 feet long..............35 cents per linear foot.
  "   over   "   "   not over 3 feet 4½ inches wide.
                            and over 4 feet long, 40 cents per linear foot.

THESE PRICES INCLUDE PACKING.

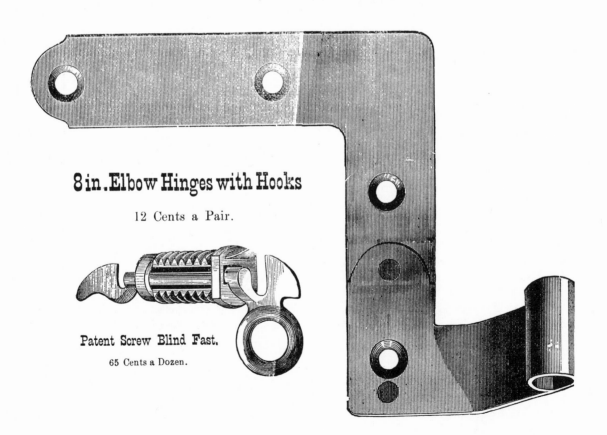

8 in. Elbow Hinges with Hooks

12 Cents a Pair.

Patent Screw Blind Fast.

65 Cents a Dozen.

KING ENAMEL PAINT.

This Paint is acknowledged by those who have used it to be a most DURABLE, BEAUTIFUL AND ECONOMICAL PAINT for either Wood, Iron, Brick, Stone or Plaster. It is suitable for all climates, as it does not *fade, chalk or peel off*, but retains its freshness and brilliancy for many years. This Paint is made from the same materials that all painters *claim* to use—*best White Lead, Zinc and Linseed Oil*—scientifically combined with other materials to increase their strength and beauty, and to improve their adhesive, durable and economical qualities. It is unequalled for outside work; the gloss, being part of its body, gives a hard enameled surface, which will resist the action of the weather longer than other paint. While the ingredients of our Paint are not new, but are the good old-fashioned articles of admitted and long tested merit, our method of mixture by machinery enables us, by thorough working, to supply a *reliable, ready-mixed Paint, of superior covering properties and of uniform tints*. One gallon of Lead and Oil Paint, mixed in the old way, will cover sixteen square yards of surface with two coats. The KING ENAMEL PAINT will cover twenty to twenty-two square yards with two coats. One gallon covers two hundred square feet, two coats, or 150 square feet 3 coats.

This Paint is sold by the gallon, and is put up in $\frac{1}{4}$, $\frac{1}{2}$ and 1 gallon cans; 5, 10 and 15 gallon kegs; also $\frac{1}{2}$ barrels and barrels. Upon application by letter, or otherwise, we will send cards with sample colors, designated by numbers, for convenience in ordering.

DIRECTIONS.

Stir thoroughly from the bottom before using. For priming use the paint of a medium thickness, not too thin (as is often recommended.) Size all knots or sappy portions. (*Putty after the first coat.*) The first coat should be thoroughly dry before the second coat is applied. Begin at the top and work downwards. Do not apply to a wet surface. Do not spread the paint too much, all it requires is to be spread evenly. Use full brush and light hand freely and evenly. Greasy places on old paint kill with lime water. Use if anything a little boiled oil in thinning.

DISCOUNT ON PRINTED PRICES TO WHOLESALE CUSTOMERS.

Subject to Changes in Market Prices of Lumber and Labor.

On O. G. Doors...........................

" Moulded Doors.....................

" Front Doors ....

" Store Doors..........................

" 12 Light Window Sash............

" 4 Light and 6 Light Window Sash.

" Irregular Sizes of Sash............

" Walnut Doors.......................

"   "   Mantels....................

" Hot Bed Sash.........................

" Window and Door Frames (put together)..........................

On Window and Door Frames (Knock Down)..............................

" Inside Shutters or Blinds.........

" Outside Panel Shutters............

" Outside Blinds......................

" Brackets and Sawed Work........

" Balusters and Newel Posts........

" White Pine Mantels and Shelves.

" Sash Weights and Cord.............

" Ornamental Glass...................

BULLETIN.

BALTIMORE, MAY, 1879.

I desire to thank my customers for their liberal patronage hitherto, and soliciting the continuance of their favors, to renew my assurances that those entrusting their orders to me shall have their interests faithfully served.

I beg also to call your attention to the accompanying PRICE LIST FOR 1879, which I propose to make the basis for all transactions during this year, regulating the same to suit any changes that there may be in the market, by the addition or deduction of a per centage. At present, to all customers, I propose to make a discount of **Sixteen and Two-Thirds Per Cent.** ($16\frac{2}{3}$) from printed prices, for **Net Cash,** (except for Ornamental Glass).

MERCHANTS and others buying large bills may obtain **SPECIAL PRICES** by application in person or by letter.

The correspondence of **DEALERS IN BUILDING MATERIALS,** and of **THOSE WHO CONTEMPLATE BUILDING** is solicited.

Very respectfully yours,

GEO. O. STEVENS.

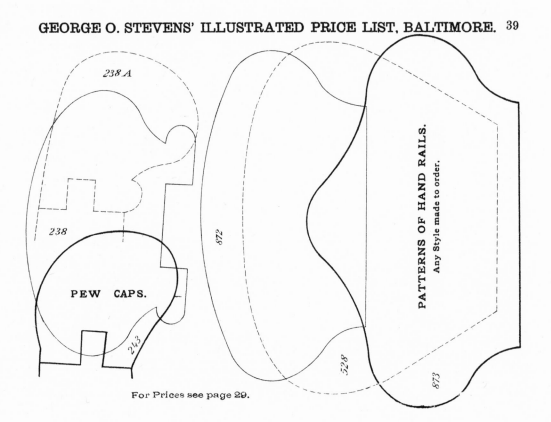

238 A

238

PEW CAPS.

243

872

528

873

PATTERNS OF HAND RAILS.
Any Style made to order.

For Prices see page 29.

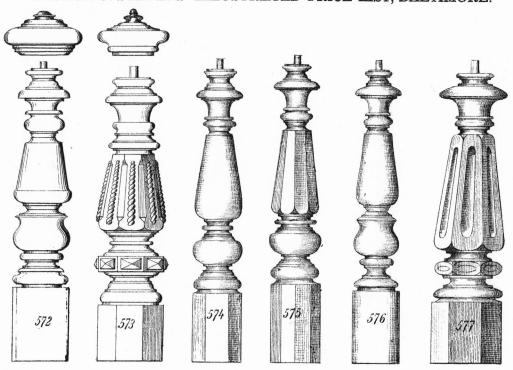

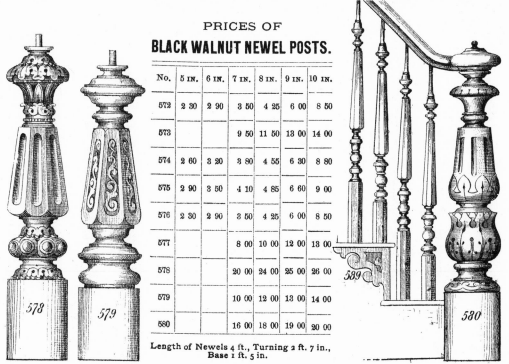

PRICES OF
BLACK WALNUT NEWEL POSTS.

No.	5 IN.	6 IN.	7 IN.	8 IN.	9 IN.	10 IN.
572	2 30	2 90	3 50	4 25	6 00	8 50
573			9 50	11 50	13 00	14 00
574	2 60	3 20	3 80	4 55	6 30	8 80
575	2 90	3 50	4 10	4 85	6 60	9 00
576	2 30	2 90	3 50	4 25	6 00	8 50
577			8 00	10 00	12 00	18 00
578			20 00	24 00	25 00	26 00
579			10 00	12 00	13 00	14 00
580			16 00	18 00	19 00	20 00

Length of Newels 4 ft., Turning 2 ft. 7 in.,
Base 1 ft. 5 in.

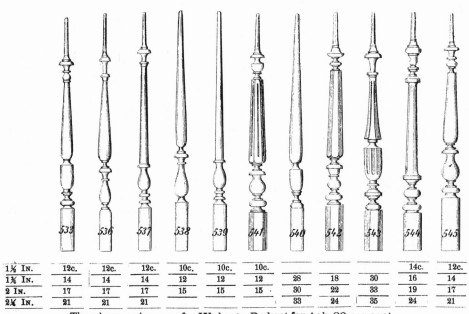

	843	842	844	845	846		548	549	550	551	552	841	840
2 In.	36c.	86c.	90c.	26c.			35c.	37c.				43	35
2¼ In.	38	88	92	28			37	40	30	30		43	35
2½ In.	40	90	1 00	30	1 20	1 10	40	43	35	35		48	40
3 In.	50	1 00	1 10	40	1 30		50	55	40	40		50	48

The above prices are for Walnut. Deduct for Ash, 15 per cent.

GEORGE O. STEVENS' ILLUSTRATED PRICE LIST, BALTIMORE. 43

	535	536	537	538	539	541	540	542	543	544	545
1½ In.	12c.	12c.	12c.	10c.	10c.	10c.				14c.	12c.
1¾ In.	14	14	14	12	12	12	28	18	30	16	14
2 In.	17	17	17	15	15	15	30	22	33	19	17
2¼ In.	21	21	21				33	24	35	24	21

The above prices are for Walnut; Deduct for Ash 20 per cent.

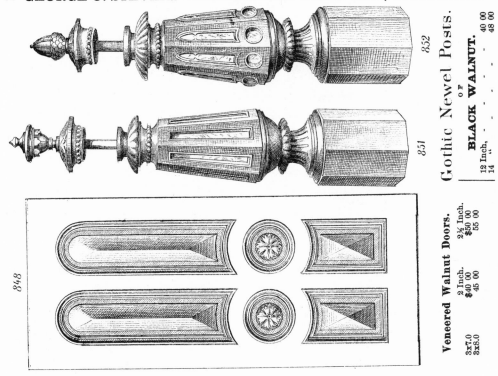

Gothic Newel Posts.
OF BLACK WALNUT.

12 Inch, - - - -	40	00
14 "	48	00

852

851

848

Veneered Walnut Doors.

	2 Inch.	2½ Inch.
3x7.0	$40 00	$50 00
3x8.0	45 00	55 00

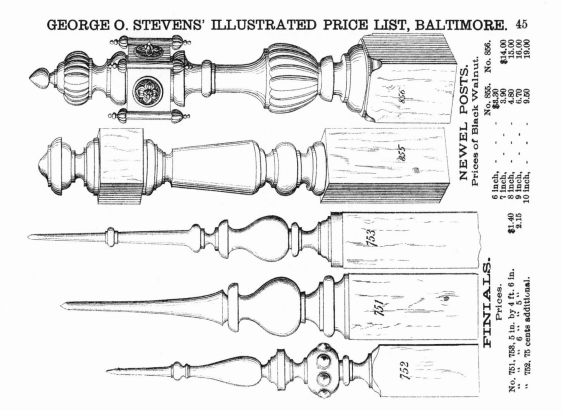

NEWEL POSTS.
Prices of Black Walnut.

	No. 855.	No. 856.
6 inch, - - - -	$3.30	$14.00
7 inch, - - - -	3.90	15.00
8 inch, - - - -	4.80	16.00
9 inch, - - - -	6.70	18.00
10 inch, - - - -	9.50	19.00

856

855

753

751

752

FINIALS.
Prices.

No. 751, 753, 5 in. by 4 ft. 6 in.	$1.40
" 752, " " 5 "	2.15
" 752, 75 cents additional.	

WHITE PINE MANTLES AND BRACKET SHELVES.

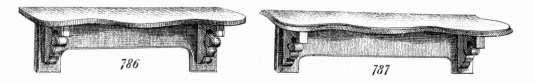

WHITE PINE MANTLES AND BRACKET SHELVES.

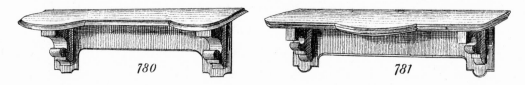

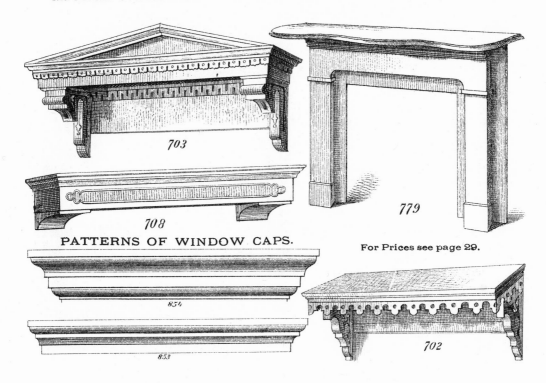

703

708

779

PATTERNS OF WINDOW CAPS.

For Prices see page 29.

854

853

702

TURNED AND SAWED CORNICE DROPS.

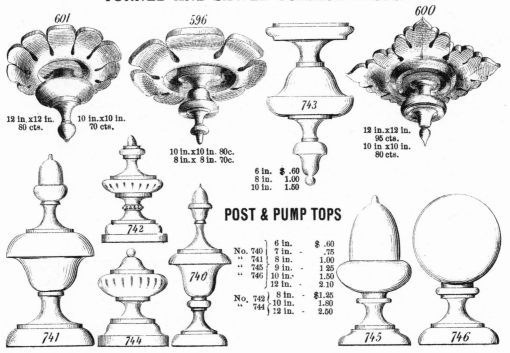

601

596

600

12 in. x12 in.
80 cts.

10 in. x10 in.
70 cts.

10 in. x10 in. 80c.
8 in. x 8 in. 70c.

743

12 in. x12 in.
95 cts.
10 in x10 in.
80 cts.

6 in. $ .60
8 in.   1.00
10 in.   1.50

742

740

POST & PUMP TOPS

No. 740 {	6 in.	$ .60
" 741 {	7 in. -	.75
" 745 {	8 in. -	1.00
" 746 {	9 in. -	1 25
	10 in. -	1.50
	12 in. -	2.10
No. 742 {	8 in. -	$1.25
" 744 {	10 in. -	1.80
	12 in. -	2.50

741

744

745

746

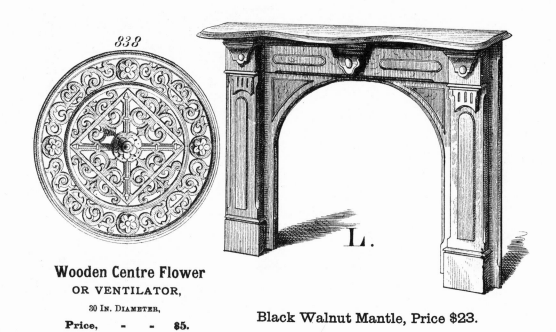

838

Wooden Centre Flower

OR VENTILATOR,

30 IN. DIAMETER,

Price,   -   - $5.

L.

Black Walnut Mantle, Price $23.

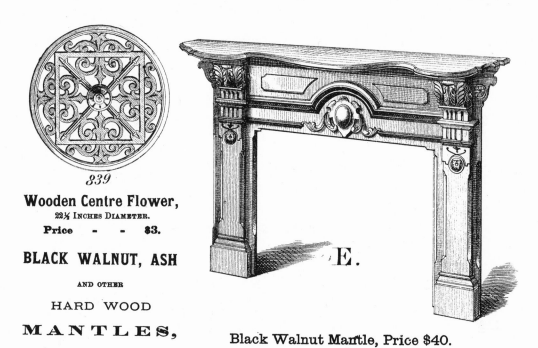

839

Wooden Centre Flower,

22½ INCHES DIAMETER.

Price   -   - $3.

BLACK WALNUT, ASH

AND OTHER

HARD WOOD

MANTLES,

Furnished to Order.

E.

Black Walnut Mantle, Price $40.

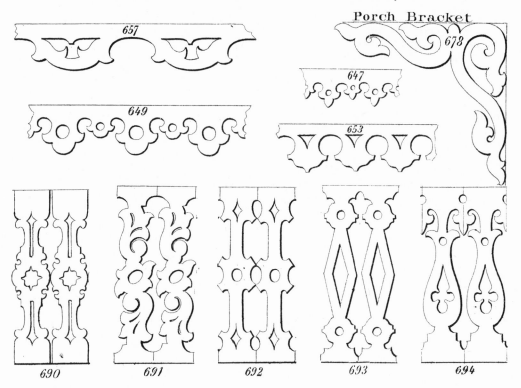

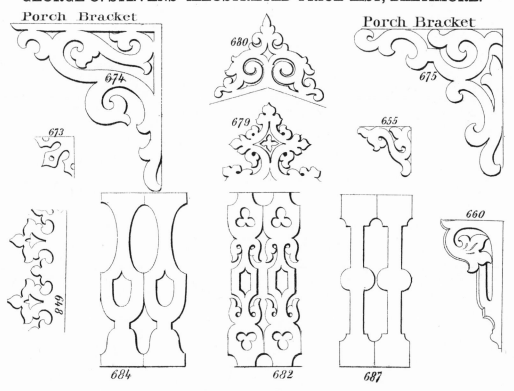

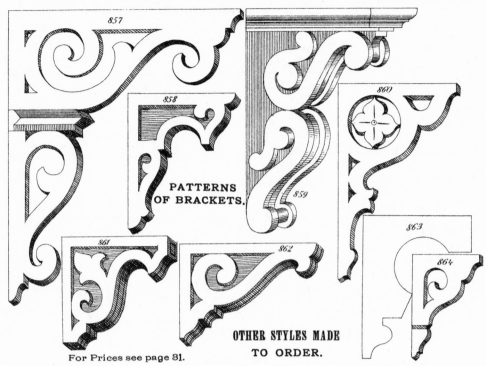

857

858

PATTERNS
OF BRACKETS.

859

860

861

862

863

864

OTHER STYLES MADE
TO ORDER.

For Prices see page 31.

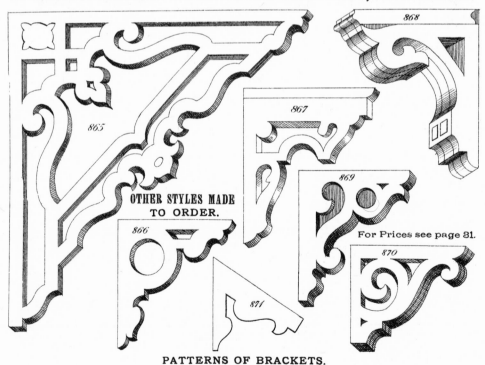

868

867

865

869

OTHER STYLES MADE
TO ORDER.

866

For Prices see page 31.

870

871

PATTERNS OF BRACKETS.

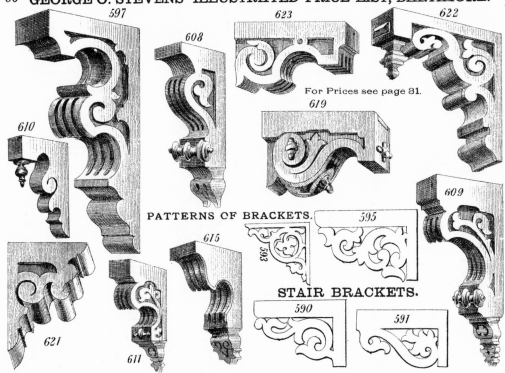

597

608

623

622

For Prices see page 31.

619

610

PATTERNS OF BRACKETS.

615

595

593

609

STAIR BRACKETS.

621

611

590

591

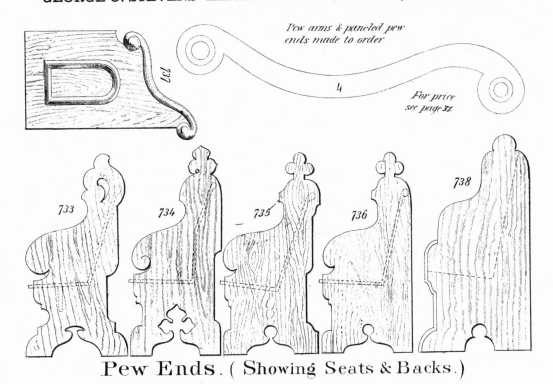

731

Pew arms & paneled pew
ends made to order

4

For price
see page 31.

733   *734*   *735*   *736*   *738*

Pew Ends. (Showing Seats & Backs.)

TURNED BALUSTRADE.

Pine or Poplar, 28 to 82 Inches Long.

	3 Inch.	4 Inch.
Nos. 551, 562, 563, 564, 565, 566, 567, 568, 569,	38 cts.	50 cts.
" 561, - - - - - -	50	60

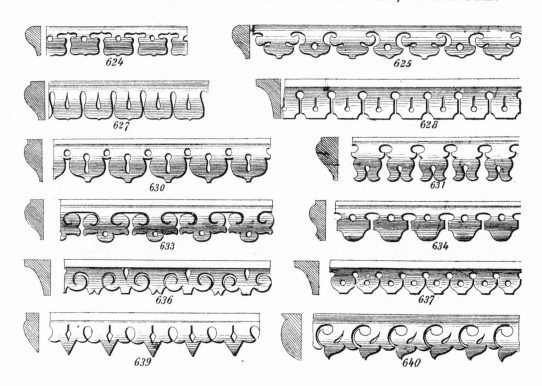

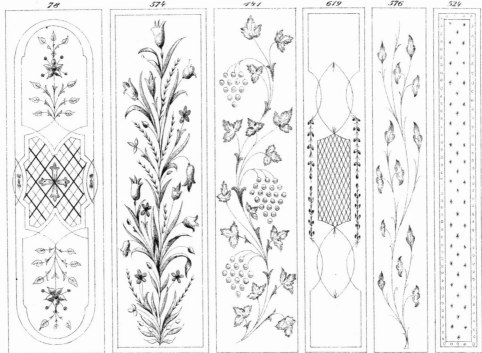

PATTERNS OF CUT AND GROUND GLASS, (Double Thick.)
For Prices see page 30.

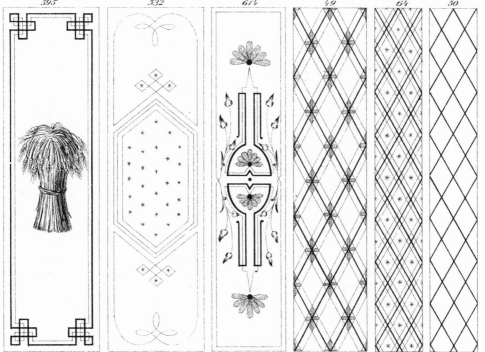

PATTERNS OF CUT AND GROUND GLASS, (Double Thick.)
For Prices see page 30.

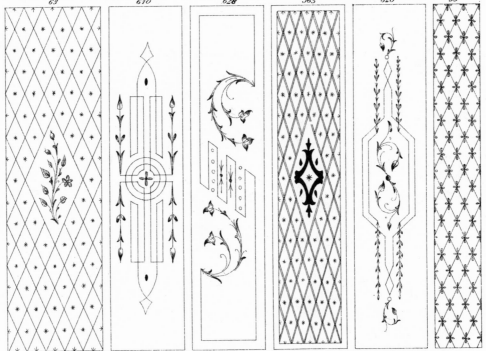

PATTERNS OF CUT AND GROUND GLASS, (Double Thick.)
For Prices see page 30.

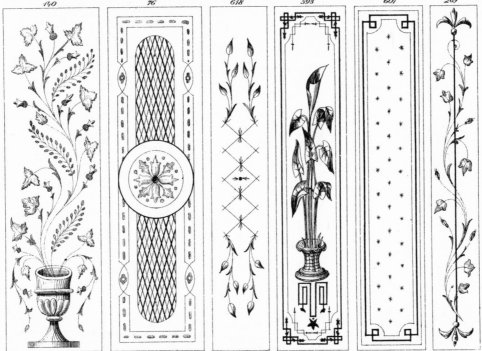

PATTERNS OF CUT AND GROUND GLASS, (Double Thick.)
For Prices see page 30.

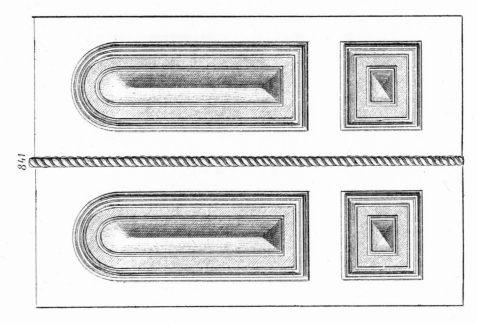

5 ft. wide x 8 ft. high or less, 2¼ in. thick. Price, $50.00.

BLACK WALNUT VENEERED DOORS IN PAIRS.

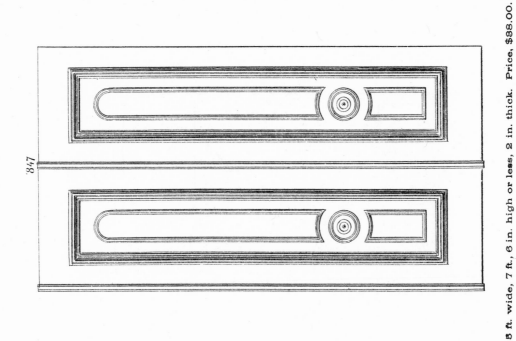

5 ft. wide, 7 ft., 6 in. high or less, 2 in. thick. Price, $38.00.

BLACK WALNUT VENEERED DOORS IN PAIRS.

4 ft. wide, 8 ft. high or less, 2 in. thick. Price, $48.00.

843

BLACK WALNUT VENEERED DOORS IN PAIRS.

For Prices see page 32.

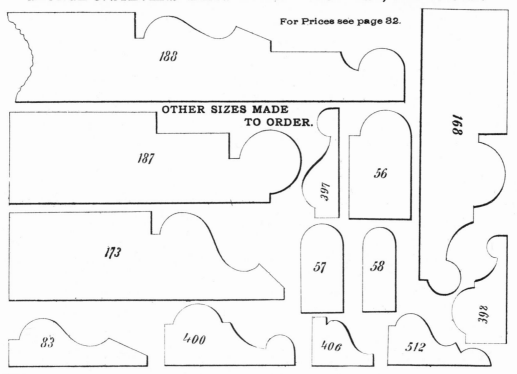

OTHER SIZES MADE
TO ORDER.

188

187

173

168

397

56

57   58

398

83   400   406   512

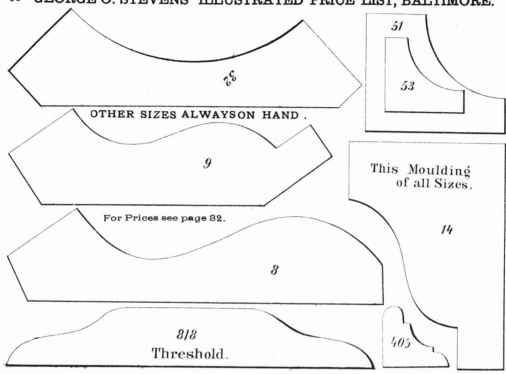

OTHER SIZES ALWAYS ON HAND.

For Prices see page 32.

This Moulding of all Sizes.

Threshold.

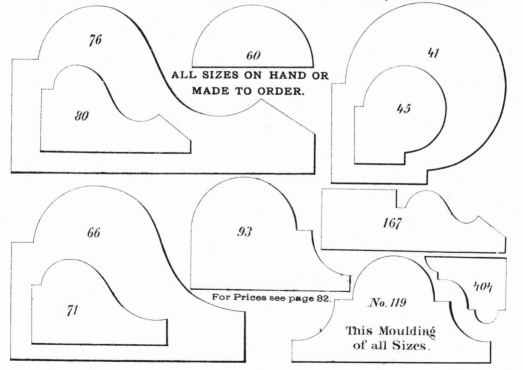

ALL SIZES ON HAND OR MADE TO ORDER.

For Prices see page 32.

This Moulding of all Sizes.

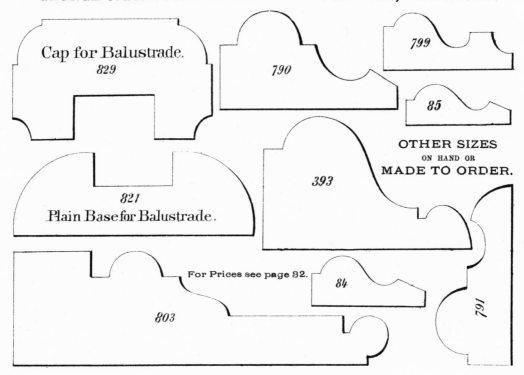

Cap for Balustrade.
829

790

799

85

OTHER SIZES
ON HAND OR
MADE TO ORDER.

821
Plain Base for Balustrade.

393

For Prices see page 32.

84

803

791